PhilanthropyRoundtable

Clearing Obstacles to Work

A Wise Giver's Guide to Fostering Self-Reliance

By David Bass

ISBN 9780986147418
LCCN 2015940349

First printing, June 2015

Current Wise Giver's Guides from The Philanthropy Roundtable

Karl Zinsmeister, *series editor*

For all current and future titles, visit PhilanthropyRoundtable.org/guidebook

TABLE OF CONTENTS

PREFACE

Just Do It—Because Work *Works*

> "A Yankee, however rich he may be, works all the time and in all
> capacities. If he is a merchant, he takes care of his store. If he is
> a farmer, he himself sows, plows, and harrows...he works side by
> side with his hired hands and eats at the same table with them. It
> seems almost incredible to the European visitor that such is the
> case, but I assure you it is true. Respect and unprecedented pas-
> sion for work—this is the invincible power of the Yankees, this
> will assure them a brilliant future and world leadership. I repeat
> once again, Yankee is synonymous with worker; be he
> millionaire or pauper, he is always a worker."

So wrote a Polish aristocrat (a kind of latter-day Tocqueville who went on
to win a Nobel Prize for literature) after he visited the United States
of America in 1876. Henryk Sienkiewicz travelled widely across our
country for several years, all the while sending dispatches back to Polish
newspapers about what he observed in this rising land. He was particularly struck by America's willingness to labor and exceptionally prescient
in predicting the great success that powerful work habits would eventually bring the young nation.

Sienkiewicz was also struck by American generosity and voluntary
philanthropy. "A man who is old and infirm, a woman, or a child, receives
more assistance in the United States than anywhere else," he observed.
Yet he noted that "a healthy young man will almost invariably hear one
piece of advice: 'Help yourself!' And if he does not know how to follow
this advice, he may even die of starvation." Along with the powerful

consensus in support of charity for the needy, there was an equally powerful American consensus that the way to hasten an able-bodied person toward a thriving existence was to lead, or push, him into energetic work.

In 2015, the American belief in work is still strong and still the source of our great successes. But there are also cracks. Whole sub-populations now exhibit a weak attachment to self-supporting labor. Researchers Isabel Sawhill and Quentin Karpilow of the liberal Brookings Institution have identified a "work gap" that puts certain families in peril. Among poor Americans, Sawhill and Karpilow report, "some households lack an employed member, a majority lack two earners, and a high proportion work very few hours even when the economy is operating at full employment."

In other words, we now have weak links in the chain of work that has long pulled Americans out of neediness and into success. Lori Sanders and Eli Lehrer of Washington's R Street Institute observe that any sensible "anti-poverty agenda today must begin with work—which presupposes employability, habits of courtesy, responsibility, punctuality, honesty, and so on. Research shows overwhelmingly that work is central to escaping poverty. This is true not only for the obvious reasons—the wages and benefits—but also for the role work plays in cultivating healthy lifestyles, helping individuals achieve self-respect, feel happier, set an example for younger generations."

Government agencies have a very checkered history when it comes to helping people who have struggled with work develop the habits and talents to do better. Statistically, most government job-training programs are quite unimpressive. There are, however, many charitable programs that have demonstrated real success at leading unskilled persons, single mothers, inexperienced minorities, released prisoners, former addicts, and other at-risk populations into lasting, transformative employment.

This book was written to help donors find those successful models and strategies. It is addressed to generous American leaders who want to lift more of our poor and distressed into mainstream success. Its purpose is to point them to the most effective work-supporting charities and approaches and to encourage them to put their shoulders to the wheel. It will be followed up next year by a second guidebook focused on what donors can do to support vocational and technical education—a field that is sometimes neglected in the push for college degrees, though it may be the most effective way for many strugglers to step onto the ladder of upward mobility (especially since employers now struggle to fill many vocational trades).

Lack of opportunity and generational progress at the bottom of our socioeconomic pyramid are now matters of concern for many Americans. The best available antidote is to help those who are lagging become effective workers. Because—as determined philanthropists in many places and all sectors have discovered—work *works* when it comes to curing deprivation, softening inequality, and erasing unhappiness.

Adam Meyerson
President, The Philanthropy Roundtable

Karl Zinsmeister
Vice president, Publications

Jo Kwong
Director, Economic Opportunity Programs

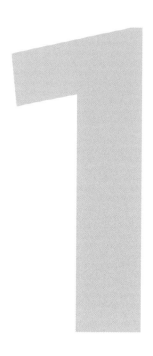

Why Work Matters

The U.S. is the richest nation in history. To see members of our society languishing in poverty, therefore, is distressing. Many of our official responses to low income, unfortunately, offer only short-term help—and even make problems worse in the long run. Government offers checks and food stamps. Philanthropy offers hot meals and shelters and donated goods. These efforts meet temporary needs. But they seldom lead to lasting improvements in the lives of strugglers, and short-term aid can become a trap.

What if we're looking in the wrong place for cures to poverty? If we cast about us to learn what it is that banishes needs and fills wants for most people, the answer is obvious: Work. That is the poverty solution that happens all around us, every day. The purpose of this guidebook is to help charitable providers lead people who are currently living at the economic margins into mainstream success and happiness through work.

Of course, work is much more than just a mechanism for reducing poverty. Our religious traditions teach that work has intrinsic value. In the Hebrew account of creation, God placed Adam in the Garden of Eden and instructed him "to work it and keep it." In the New Testament, Paul stated that "if a man will not work, he will not eat." The Calvinist work ethic brought to our shores by the Puritans equated diligent work with duty to God.

More than any other nation on Earth, the United States has a rich tradition of insisting that hard work is ennobling. In our country—unlike others—even the most mundane occupations have been viewed as bringing honor to the laborer. And this has helped every succeeding generation of Americans enjoy a brighter economic future than the one before it.

The American experience with work stands counter to most of human history. For centuries, work was a compulsory drudgery, essential for survival but seldom leading to clear and lasting improvements in living conditions. In the dynamic American economy, work effort translated much more predictably and reliably into prosperity. Work brought tangible outcomes, often quickly, that could be savored, shared, and used to build a future for one's family, community, and the nation as a whole.

These twin benefits of the American work ethic—material betterment and a sense of personal value—have sometimes been lost sight of in recent years and are no longer experienced by all of our citizens. Amid new ideas of entitlement and guaranteed outcomes, and expanded notions of retirement and disability, there are pockets where the virtues of work are no longer understood or appreciated, or where residents have become entangled in dribbling payment programs that make active employment almost impossible. Moreover, specific jobs used as stepping stones by many people in the past have disappeared due to technological change or economic globalism. There are spatial mismatches, skill gaps, and missing habits, attitudes, and experiences that separate workers from work.

Of the 27 million persons of working age (18-64) who fell below the poverty line in 2013, 16 million didn't hold a job for even one week during the year. So simply going to work is the first step they (and their dependents) most need. Among the 10 million prime-age persons who were poor though they did work, some lacked the requisite skills to support themselves, but most just put in too few hours to sustain a household.

Diligent work is not something innately wired into human beings. It must be taught, cultivated, and practiced. It is a skill set, like any other, that must be pursued. Offering employment tools and productive attitudes toward work and self-support is a fertile field for charitable donors.

Good charitable organizations do a better job at linking the disadvantaged with careers than government agencies. They are more personal and less bureaucratic. They have no guaranteed budgets, so they only survive if they produce results. They often look far beyond initial job offers to seek ways of life that will be durable for the people they help.

Unlike government agencies, private civil-society groups are free to address issues of character, personal behavior, virtue, and habit without risking a lawsuit. Many of these organizations bring moral insights to their job training, as well as community values, and faith angles, knowing that they have no coercive powers over clients who voluntarily choose to participate. Their offerings are often about a renewed life, a second chance, days of purpose—not just a job.

In this guidebook we'll highlight scores of local nonprofits that have good records of helping marginal populations become happily employed. We'll discover what succeeds and what doesn't. Donors, charitable practitioners, and pioneering thinkers will explain triumphs and failures in their own words and describe, from experience, the lives they've seen deflected from misery and dependence toward productivity and fulfillment.

This book explores in detail the practices that have produced results with seven important populations that particularly struggle with work:

- Single parents on assistance
- Released prisoners
- The homeless
- Substance abusers
- The disabled
- The unskilled
- Disconnected youth

These are some of the hardest-to-reach populations in the U.S. right now. They offer donors a chance to set in motion major life improvements.

In this field it is possible for wise philanthropists to change individual fortunes dramatically—and to alter entire family trees for the better. That is the purpose of this guidebook.

Benefits of a work-filled life

Everyone needs income to survive, but meaningful work is about far more than the paycheck. Work establishes the daily rhythms of life. It dictates when we rise from bed, when we eat our meals, how we schedule our weeks, how we interact with our families. Work provides important structure for our lives.

Work also forms the backbone of much of our social interaction. This has become increasingly true in recent decades as Americans have slid away from many forms of traditional community and civic participation, leaving the workplace as their primary locale of social engagement. Much of our identity now comes from our work. Asked what we "do," we name our day job, even though that constitutes only a portion of our identity.

> Meaningful work is about far more than the paycheck. Work establishes the daily rhythms and structure of life.

"A job doesn't define who you are, but it does give you a sense of purpose for waking up every day," says Sandy Schultz, CEO of WorkFaith Connection, a work-bolstering organization based in Houston, Texas. "Having a job helps people to see that they are valuable. It's hugely significant." Peter Droege, executive director of the drug-rehabilitation program Step 13, says "we're much more than what we do for a living, but the fact remains that work is ennobling."

Everyone benefits from honest work—not just the employee who gets paid, not just his company that reaps benefits. Diligent work allows many people to profit from the services, products, ideas, or advancements produced. Good work is built around solving the problems of others and reaping a reward for doing so, and thus helps society as a whole.

For many, work is a cause beyond themselves, even a life calling. This can be as true for simple jobs as for complex ones. Work gives everyone a chance to put a proud personal stamp on the world.

When they are separated from work, the poor lose more than just money for food, shelter, and clothing. They suffer deficits of purpose, emotional well-being, and social connection. They get cut off from clearly defined goals and aspirations. They lose a prime means of generating and feeling respect from others. These things can't be compensated for by government income transfers or charitable gifts. This itch must be scratched by devoting oneself to productive, fulfilling labor.

A premise of this guidebook is that human beings are most satisfied when they enjoy the material, emotional, and spiritual fruits of their own toil. Philanthropists can play a key role in making this happen.

Authors Steve Corbett and Brian Fikkert explore this issue in *When Helping Hurts: How to Alleviate Poverty Without Hurting the Poor...and Yourself*. Their experience is in international Christian missions in underdeveloped nations, but their insights apply to poor populations in the U.S. as well. One of the major dilemmas exposed by Corbett and Fikkert is the disconnect between what givers believe poor people need and what poor people themselves actually want. Wealthy observers, they note, "describe poverty differently than the poor in low-income countries do," tending "to emphasize a lack of material things such as food, money, clean water, medicine, housing, etc." Meanwhile, poor people

> tend to describe their condition in far more psychological and social terms.... Poor people typically talk in terms of shame, inferiority, powerlessness, humiliation, fear, hopelessness, depression, social isolation, and voicelessness.... This mismatch between many outsiders' perceptions of poverty and the perceptions of poor people themselves can have devastating consequences for poverty-alleviation efforts.

The advantage of work is that it provides an antidote both to poverty and to depression. In addition to yielding goods, it opens broad avenues to participation and meaning.

Carla Javits, executive director of the San Francisco-based venture-philanthropy fund REDF, has encountered in her own work the mix of physical and psychological needs of the jobless. REDF specializes in creating and supporting businesses that employ the most difficult-to-reach populations, such as the homeless and drug addicts. She told us:

When you ask the people we're helping why they are so excited to have a job, you'd think the first thing they would say is the pay-check—because we're talking about people who are extremely low-income. Yet they almost never give that as their first answer. It's almost always dignity, self-respect, participation, team, and community. It's really profound to think of that.

In the United States, we believe in work. We believe in the power of work. If you're left out of that, you feel like you're left out of the whole society. Many people who have fallen out of mainstream society come to a moment in their life when they're ready to make major personal changes to get back in and be part of that American dream. A job is the ticket back in—it's your on-ramp back into the mainstream of society.

Unfortunately, after you've been withdrawn from work for a while, it can sometimes be really tough to find a path to return.

Although they emphasize the importance of material relief, Corbett and Fikkert identify changed attitudes as the surest path to poverty reduction, beginning with those who wish to help. Proper thinking requires "more than ensuring that people have sufficient material things; rather, it involves the much harder task of empowering people to earn sufficient material things through their own labor, for in so doing we move people closer to being what God created them to be."

The struggle for donors is this: Too many poverty-alleviation efforts provide material relief to the exclusion of other goals. Even charitable organizations that place the impoverished in jobs sometimes end up providing only stopgap help, because broader life changes are not achieved. An impossible family situation, creditors on your back, a lack of reliable transportation, no connection to social capital, few educational resources, lack of role models, lack of financial knowledge, a negative worldview—addressing these at the same time one works will make success much more likely. Too many of the poor and impoverished are in survival mode rather than advancement mode. A charitable support structure can help solve or soften concerns that could otherwise get in the way of finding and holding a job.

Paradoxically, opportunities to give and serve others are another thing often missing from the life of the poor. Feeling valuable to fellow human beings is a fundamental part of flourishing. Lots of research shows that givers are the happiest people on the planet. Work provides many chances to contribute and be a blessing to others.

In the end, work helps to create an intangible quality of character that few other activities can: self respect. Philanthropist and entrepreneur David Weekley identifies that as one of the distinguishing aspects of good work. "From what I've seen, giving people a hand up rather than a handout is the only way to create self respect and permanent improvement in people's lives, rather than temporary improvement," he told us in an interview. "That's what I feel called to do: help folks, over the long-term, change their lives."

Why donors should care about work

In his book *From Prophecy to Charity: How to Help the Poor*, economist Lawrence Mead notes that 12 percent of the U.S. population was classified as impoverished in 2009, and the poverty rate for non-working persons stood at 23 percent. Yet for people who put in any work at all during the year, the poverty rate was 7 percent, and for those who worked at least a 35-hour workweek for 50 weeks of the year—at any job—the poverty rate was just 3 percent.

The power of work can be seen internationally as well, especially when whole communities transition to productive labor. Peter Greer, CEO of Hope International, outlines the relevant numbers in his book *Stop Helping Us! A Call to Compassionately Move Beyond Charity*:

> Between 1981 and 2005...the number of people living in extreme poverty ($1.25 or less per day) decreased from 52 percent to 26 percent. In one generation, poverty has been cut in half, not through charity but through job creation.... For example, in 1981, 84 percent of China's population lived below the poverty line... by 2005, the percentage dropped to 25 percent. During this timeframe, China's GDP increased tenfold. Brazil and India followed the same path...the changes being powered by economic growth.

A chief differentiation between people who thrive and those who struggle is that successful people are active workers. It doesn't happen instantly. But those who successfully attach themselves to work, develop a career path, and seek to improve their skills and knowledge base, almost always end their lives with economic success.

In emphasizing the long-term importance of work, it's not our intention to dismiss or ignore charity work that provides immediate material relief to the poor—such as food pantries, rescue missions, and homeless shelters. After all, it's hard to get a stable job when you're hungry and don't know where you will sleep that night. Many donors consider it a religious or moral imperative to supply relief in the face of sharp need.

"But it's not either/or—teach a man to fish or give a man a fish," says Hugh Whelchel, director of the Institute for Faith, Work & Economics. "If you try to teach a man to fish and he's starving, then he's going to eat the bait. So there has got to be this immediate relief where we help people get stabilized. But that's got to be followed very quickly by a way to help him begin to use the gifts and opportunities that God has given him to provide for himself."

> For people who worked at least a 35-hour workweek for 50 weeks of the year—at any job—the poverty rate was just 3 percent.

The hundreds of thousands of meals that charitable food pantries and soup kitchens serve to the homeless and impoverished each day are essential work. But the premise of this book is that a fuller approach is necessary, adding a lasting focus on lifting the impoverished into self-production, gradual accumulation of wealth, and personal security.

Here are three more reasons, pragmatic ones, why donors should get involved in the long-term work of helping the dependent find jobs:

- **Collective prosperity**
  A larger pool of useful workers benefits society as a whole. Workers generate value, pay taxes, they support themselves rather than hanging on others, their families are healthier, they are less prone to crime.
- **Building freedom**
  People with jobs can more easily choose where they live, what they eat, how they school their children, and so forth. They can exercise freedom in practice, not just in theory, in our land of liberty.
- **Lasting results**
  People with unsuccessful work histories become mired in generational poverty, something much worse than the temporary misfortunes that all of us are at risk of occasionally experiencing.

Transforming a dependent person into a worker can transform a whole family line for the better.

Dan Rose helped design the Kindle, became a Facebook vice president, then became interested in philanthropy in 2011. He helps fund and serves on the board of directors of REDF, one of the leading charities guiding economic strugglers into work they can be proud of. "The social chain is only as strong as its weakest link," he says, which is why "we need to help lift people up. A job is the single most important thing for someone to become a productive member of society. It's much more than just an income: it's a sense of pride, a sense of contributing. A sense of being a father or a mother who your kids can look up to and admire. All of those things come with having a job."

The Troubling Decline of Work

The U.S. remains a land of opportunity, where hard work is generally well rewarded. That's the good news. The bad news: mushrooming expansion of the welfare state (especially in areas like disability compensation and food assistance), a devastating recession followed by an anemic recovery, barriers to entry for challenged populations, and broad degradation of the work ethic have combined to depress work levels in the U.S. rather dramatically in recent decades. This chapter will explore reasons for the troubling decline in work, building understanding of the practical tools, methods, and approaches that donors need to apply to counteract these trends.

The labor market tells the story

One doesn't need to look far to see evidence of our employment problems. Beaten down by the Great Recession, only 52 percent of Americans told the Gallup poll in 2013 that they think our country currently has plenty of opportunity—down from 81 percent in 1998. Unemployment rates and evidence of stagnating wages receive ample media attention. What more often is pushed to the side is the decline of work itself. A core economic problem in the U.S. today is that a significant fraction of Americans who could be working aren't, and that number has steadily grown in recent years.

After reaching a high of 10 percent in October 2009, the U.S. unemployment rate dropped to 5.6 percent by the spring of 2015. This would seem to be cause for celebration. A more thorough examination of the numbers, however, reveals that a major reason for that decline was that many able persons simply dropped out of the workforce. The government's so-called U-6 unemployment rate adds to the official jobless the underemployed and those who have basically stopped looking for employment. In the spring of 2015—a full five years after the end of the last recession—the U-6 unemployment rate stood at 11 percent.

Even more telling is the ratio of persons who are currently employed to those who are of working age. This is called the labor force participation rate. We know there has been a major move into the labor force by women over the last generation. What is not generally understood is that male workers have been falling out of the productive workforce during that same time.

Research from the U.S. Bureau of Labor Statistics (after carefully adjusting for complicating factors like the aging of our population) shows that while 83 percent of all working-age men held down a job in 1960, the same ratio had fallen to 75 percent by the year 2000 when the U.S. economy was at a peak. In the years since, it has edged down even more—with the result that more than a quarter of prime-age males are now not even trying to work. This withdrawal of men from the labor market stands in sharp contrast to the traditional American experience of manhood, which was closely tied to gainful employment. One of the reasons for our lackluster recovery from the Great Recession has been a declining pool of men eager to find a job—any job.

Low-income and blue-collar men have led the retreat. "In the 1960 census, about 9 percent of all [blue-collar] men ages 20-64 were not in the labor force," writes sociologist Charles Murray in his book *Coming Apart*. "In the 2000 census, about 30 percent of [blue-collar] men in the same age range were not in the labor force."

Even young people are dropping out. Between 2002 and 2012, labor force participation by individuals between the ages of 16 and 24 fell by more than eight percentage points. The drop was even starker among teenagers—over 13 percentage points. In 2012, the Social Science Research Council reported that 14 percent of all Americans age 16-24, and 26 percent of African-American men in that age block, were neither in school nor in a job.

It is work that has powered the American experience of upward mobility and a better life for each succeeding generation. With our rate and intensity of work in decline, it's no wonder that Americans feel pessimistic about future economic improvement. A 2014 NBC-Wall Street Journal poll found that 76 percent of respondents didn't feel confident that life for their children's generation would be better than it was for their own generation.

The role of dependence in our work slump

Reasons for the decline of work in the U.S. are multifaceted and complex. One of the biggest culprits is government intervention itself. Though well intentioned, welfare payments of various sorts have become a serious barrier to securing self-sufficient employment. The famous Seattle/Denver Income Maintenance Experiment, carefully conducted to discover what would happen if the government guaranteed incomes to Americans, found that for every $1 of extra state transfers given to low-income persons, they reduced their labor earnings by 80 cents.

Income transfers have become a mainstream phenomenon in the U.S.—as middle class as a suburban house, two-car garage, and pet dog. The latest ratcheting up was the arrival of the Patient Protection and Affordable Care Act, which allows, for example, a family of four earning up to $95,400 per year to qualify for health-care subsidies. But well before health-care reform, transfer payments had become common in the middle class. American Enterprise Institute economist Nick Eberstadt writes:

> Over 49 percent of America's population lived in households that were using at least one government benefit to help support

themselves in early 2011. This represented a tremendous increase over the early 1980s, at which time just under 30 percent of Americans were estimated to live in homes drawing entitlements from at least one of the government's many benefit programs.... A majority of American voters live in homes now applying for and obtaining one or more benefits from U.S. government programs.

Nearly every expert, service provider, and philanthropist interviewed for this guidebook agreed on one point: government assistance is now one of the largest factors blocking hurting populations from escaping a listless existence. Private organizations can encourage healthy work and personal responsibility. But they often must battle incentives not to work rising from readily available transfers.

The problem is not confined to traditional welfare payments, food stamps, and government-provided housing. Consider the dramatic rise in government-provided disability payments. Even as the U.S. population enjoys much safer workplaces, new medical cures, expanded legal protection and services for the disabled across society, plus astonishing

> Between 1983 and 2003, average work input for those lacking a high-school degree slipped from 44 to 33 hours per week for men, and from 18 to 15 for women.

adaptive technology, dependence on disability subsidies has jumped dramatically. In *Unfit for Work: The Startling Rise of Disability in America,* Chana Joffe-Walt reports that 14 million Americans now receive a disability check from the government each month. "The federal government spends more money each year on cash payments for disabled former workers than it spends on food stamps and welfare combined." The Social Security Administration reports that since the beginning of the Great Recession in 2007, the rate of those receiving disabled-worker benefits has jumped by 26 percent.

The spike in the number of workers who consider themselves disabled is a major factor in falling labor force participation. Lax systems now allow disability payments without much scrutiny, without any expectation that the recipient will pursue medical treatment, without inventiveness in seeking workforce accommodations, indeed with built-in ratchets that cause many recipients who go on the rolls with modest disabilities to continually expand their claims until they are considered fully and irreclaimable disabled for life. For lower-skilled workers, disability payments can now seem more enticing than a job.

Working but struggling to make ends meet

So far, we have established that work rates and labor force participation have declined in the U.S. over the past several decades. What about the Americans who are working yet still finding it hard to pay their bills each month? What are the reasons for this, and are solutions available? Understanding the needs of the working poor begins with knowing that their main problem today is usually the number of hours worked.

Historically, rich Europeans and Asians often lived parasitically off inherited land and the toil of others, eschewing and even disdaining sustained work of their own. In modern societies, that pattern is inverted. Today most wealthy persons work very long hours, and it is the poor who exhibit intermittent or non-existent work.

For over a century, the 40-hour workweek has characterized American economic life, and for many it's seen as a minimum rather than a goal. The U.S. as a whole prides itself on working far longer hours than our Western European counterparts. Lower-income workers, however, tend to put far less time into work, involuntarily or by choice. Today, those who labor longest at workplaces are rarely the poor; they tend to be in the higher income brackets.

Here again, government has played a role in shifting behavior. Income limitations on many transfer payments have the perverse incentive of reducing hours on the job of persons who might otherwise put in a full 40-hour workweek. Maria Kim—president of Cara, a top-rated work-supporting nonprofit in Chicago—reports that dealing with the loss of government benefits is now a big issue for people transitioning from dependence to work. "Typically in the first six months of someone being in gainful employment, if they've had public subsidies, they will lose almost all of them," Kim says. The so-called "cliff effect" where benefits turn off at a certain income level can lead clients to limit hours or upside career potential in order to maintain government transfers.

The work-hours disparity is seen clearly in time-use surveys. An analysis by economists Mark Aguiar and Erik Hurst found that between

1983 and 2003, average work hours per week for those lacking a high-school degree slipped from 44 to 33 for men, and from 18 to 15 for women. Among the college-educated over that same period, work hours increased from an average of 42 to 45 hours per week for men, and from 26 to 31 hours per week for women.

Some workers put in a full 40-hour workweek and still can't escape poverty—but their numbers are small. Only 2.7 percent of Americans who work full time, year-round, are in poverty. Among households that fall in the lowest 20 percent by income, only 11 percent of the heads work full time, year-round. If you look at poor families with children in the U.S., you find that the family is supported by an average of only 16 working hours per week. If each poor family had just one full-time worker, three quarters of today's poor children would be lifted out of poverty.

"The poor have less income in large measure because they work far fewer hours than their more affluent counterparts," write Isabel Sawhill and Ron Haskins of the Brookings Institution. With limited work hours being the major problem, raising the minimum wage can have only

> If each poor family in the U.S. had just one full-time worker, three quarters of today's poor children would be lifted out of poverty.

limited effects. Moreover, as New York University economist Lawrence Mead points out, "most minimum wage workers are not heads of household and are not poor. They live in families where other people are working. Nor do most poor adults, when they do work, earn only the minimum wage. They typically earn somewhat above that. They are poor mainly due to low working levels, not low wages."

Donors who want to serve the poor effectively must focus on helping them devote themselves to jobs—encouraging the life stability, attitudes, and home conditions that will allow full-time work, and the skills and consistency to earn a living wage on their own. These are things that the best private workforce-development organizations profiled in this book focus on intently. Many are able to produce clear successes. Donors make it all possible, and with more donations these effective programs can be expanded and copied in needy cities across the nation.

Overcoming the biggest barriers to work

Self-discipline. Cooperation. Responsibility. Constructive attitudes. These factors are the foundation of a healthy work ethic, and have always been the crucial underpinnings of economic success. Philanthropists today need to help rebuild these prerequisites of occupational achievement.

Cincinnati Works is a nonprofit (profiled in the next chapter) that has been very successful at providing job-readiness training and ongoing career guidance to people who have failed at self-support in the past. When they were founding the organization in the mid-1990s, donors David and Liane Phillips discovered that among the chronically jobless population they wanted to boost up, the main problems were not economics.

> Every one of the people we sought to help had some barrier keeping them from finding a decent job. What we failed to anticipate was that almost every one of them ran up against multiple barriers. Nobody had just one.

Here are nine common barriers to work identified by the scores of donors and experts interviewed for this guidebook:

1. Skills gaps

In many entry-level jobs, a chasm now exists between what employers want and what prospective employees bring to the table. This applies not only to technical knowledge but "soft skills," such as time management and respect for supervisors. According to 42 percent of employers queried in a recent national survey, many high-school graduates now entering our job force lack the capacities needed to succeed in a modern workplace.

2. Long-term unemployment

The longer one goes without a job, the more difficult it is to find and succeed at one. In 2014, 3.2 million Americans were considered "long-term unemployed" (meaning they had been jobless for 27 weeks or more). That is one third of all unemployed persons. These individuals will find it difficult to acquire and hold employment.

3. Increased competition

The Great Recession and the anemic recovery since have increased competition for job opportunities. This problem is likely to solve itself if more growth-oriented economic policies are instituted, but at the moment many baby boomers who would otherwise have retired are continuing work to rebuild their retirement savings, reducing new openings for young people. Contra the broad declines in labor-force participation sketched earlier, older Americans are the one group now swimming in the other direction. From 2002 to 2012, persons 55 and over increased their partic-ipation rate from 35 percent to 41 percent, the only age group to do so.

4. Changing economy

Globalization and shifts from manufacturing to a service- and knowl-edge-based economy mean that many men who once labored successfully in blue-collar positions do not have employable talents.

5. A culture of dependence

"I can't tell you how many times I've had conversations with women who, while they were growing up, didn't know anybody who worked," says Tamra Ryan, CEO of the Women's Bean Project, a social enterprise based in Denver that creates starting jobs for marginalized women. The project has found that establishing a different social circle where positive rather than negative values are reinforced is crucial. "Work ethic and soft skills…the overall culture of poverty—they are all a big part of the challenge," agrees Peggy Zink, presi-dent of Cincinnati Works. "How can we help people move to the culture of the middle class? Sometimes it takes successive failures in jobs to learn."

6. Soaring single-parenthood

Stable marriages and dual-parent childraising lead to much better eco-nomic outcomes all around. Children in married families are vastly less likely to face economic and emotional struggles. Single mothers of young children have great difficulty working, paying for childcare, and balancing time demands. Unmarried fathers are vastly less successful at work compared to otherwise identical married counterparts. Statistically, married couples with at least one spouse working full time are almost never in poverty. With marriage rates now reaching all-time lows, and half of all children spending time in a single-parent family, there are inevitable economic penalties.

7. Criminal backgrounds

About 650,000 inmates are released from U.S. prisons each year. Rebuild-ing a rewarding, virtuous life that includes work is not easy after time behind bars. Many ex-offenders return to criminality and incarceration.

8. Drug and alcohol abuse

Close to ten percent of Americans took illicit drugs in the latest year. Many others abuse alcohol. These behaviors interfere with work habits, productivity, public safety, and family life. Many thousands of employees are terminated each year for drug- and alcohol-related infractions.

9. Homelessness

Homeless persons generally have spotty or non-existent work histories which turn their résumés into flashing warning signs for employers. They lack settled addresses where they can be contacted. Their hygiene, clothing, and food consumption are often unconducive to being hired and participating in a workplace. Lack of means of transportation is frequently an issue. These things make the homeless hard to employ.

Despite deeply rooted obstacles like those spelled out here, many workforce charities have found that economic strugglers can be converted to successful jobholders—if they are willing to take on the mantle of responsible employee, and handed the right tools. "People are moved from desperation and belief in the welfare system as their only option to understanding that they can succeed," says Harriet Karr-McDonald, co-founder of the Doe Fund, a homeless-to-work program in New York City. Eldridge Gray, long-time funder of the youth entrepreneurship organization BUILD, suggests that "earning a paycheck and achieving financial well-being are universally appealing."

Why donors should help strugglers surmount barriers

Many of the philanthropists who help chip away at the barriers described in this chapter are successful businesspeople who want to devote part of their fortune to ensuring that paths to self-sufficiency remain open for any economic struggler willing to commit himself to transformation and self-improvement. There are also foundations that loyally fund in this area. The Harry and Jeanette Weinberg, Annie E. Casey, Adolph Coors, Farmer Family, Frey, Anschutz, and Abell foundations are just a few leading examples. Despite the lack of glamour, and the significant dropout rates attendant to this kind of work, these donors offer support again and again because they know that the individuals who do succeed (and for the successful groups it is often more than half of the troubled folks who start), the transformation can be dramatic, lasting, and transmitted to the next generation. That's why helping at-risk populations become persistent workers is an expanding area of philanthropy.

Asked why donors should invest in workforce growth, George Roberts, founder of the finance giant Kohlberg Kravis Roberts & Co. and creator of the very successful venture-philanthropy fund REDF, encourages philanthropists to personalize the issue. "Just think for a minute if you didn't have a job," he urges. "No one wanted to hire you. You had no hope for a job. You were taken care of because of the public system, but people didn't want you. Just think what that must be like to somebody. They don't have hope, really. Put yourself in that person's shoes for a second and ask yourself what it would be like. Then I think it's possible to see how worthwhile it is to help these people."

Good programs offer more than a job; they offer a new and better life. And they are able to convince participants that achieving such a life is within a person's grasp. "If you're going to attract marginal populations to work, one of the keys is to demonstrate that success is possible," says Tom Owens, an entrepreneur, philanthropist, and head of the Owens Foundation in Chicago.

> There is a spiritual or psychological aspect that keeps people poor. What a lot of these great programs do is help people see what they can achieve.

Don MacKenzie is a real-estate developer, donor, and chairman of the Denver-based Center for Work Education and Employment, a nonprofit that helps welfare-dependent women transition to work. He acknowledges that many other worthy philanthropic goals exist for donors. "But in terms of trying to get more of our society producing than receiving, what is more important than job training?" he asks.

Donn Weinberg, executive vice president of Baltimore's Harry and Jeanette Weinberg Foundation, is a strong advocate for donor involvement in workforce training. He sees it as the best solution to lifting the poor into lasting success. "Employment is at the center of our philosophy," he says. The foundation's original wealth creator, Harry Weinberg, grew up poor in Baltimore, then built a transportation and real-estate empire. He believed a strong work ethic was the key to a better life, and left most of his money to support earned upward mobility. With $2 billion in assets, the Weinberg Foundation invests about $100 million each year in helping the poor and vulnerable.

Some of the foundation's cornerstone investments include $15 million to build up the tough-love job program STRIVE between 2002 and 2014; $2 million for the Cara Program in Chicago; $2 million of steady support for Year Up; and recent aid for Seattle's FareStart effort. Weinberg suggests that fellow donors interested in workforce development should find a nonprofit in their area that offers good job training and attend the first day of a new class. Then come back on the final days when participants are graduating. The difference you will see in many of the men and women will be palpable, he says.

"If a donor is looking for something inspiring, something he can feel," says Weinberg, "this will be truly heartwarming. These people are not only getting jobs and potentially moving up the economic ladder—they're learning what to do with their lives."

"There is a spiritual or psychological aspect that keeps people poor," Weinberg argues. "In order to have a shot, you must have hope for the future. You must believe that if you engage in the effort to improve, it will be fruitful. If you believe that no matter what you do it won't make a difference, then why get started? What a lot of these great programs do is help people see what they can achieve."

Teaching the Skills of Life Transformation

Very often, the biggest gaps that separate strugglers from people who are successful fall in the area of "soft skills"—the nuts and bolts that make it possible for a worker to be effective on the job: showing up on time, listening well to instructions, being reliable, keeping one's temper even when pressed, having a positive attitude, dressing appropriately, using work-appropriate language, accepting constructive criticism, not blaming others for failures, finishing work on time.

Strugglers often must learn these traits in the workplace because they didn't master them at home. That's why charitable programs put an emphasis on social skills, timekeeping and scheduling, emotional self-mastery, and avoiding negative influences. The organizations featured in this guidebook strengthen these soft skills by not only teaching them through coursework but also by demanding them in practice—putting program participants on a tight schedule, requiring respect, demanding promptness and completion of assignments. The best programs tend to be tough and taxing, with instructors sternly challenging slack or anti-social behavior.

A job applicant whose soft skills are evident will be taken seriously by companies, Donn Weinberg stresses, even if his technical skills are rusty. "What employers need is someone who is ready to work—ready with the soft skills that then allow them to absorb the hard skills," he says. "When you're at the job, it's not about you. It's about the customer or satisfying the boss, which means you have to really listen and understand."

In this chapter, we'll plumb the most promising techniques for effectively instructing those who lack these basic necessities. Character training, classroom instruction, hands-on experience, entrepreneurial challenges, practical follow-up—these are combined in programs that lead people from previous failures in the job market to steady work. Successful models typically have intensive, highly structured programs. They place serious demands on participants, including a willingness to flunk out non-cooperators. Highly developed job-placement services, and ongoing reinforcement and support from program staff and alumni are usually central.

At their core, most of these organizations are structured around a simple concept: If you're currently living off someone else, crave an escape from low-income misery, want to do things you and your family will be proud of, and are willing to work hard, then we'll help you find a job and establish a career. If you think you can get these things without thoroughly (often painfully) changing the way you have lived up until now, sorry—come back and see us when you are committed to true life transformation.

Cincinnati Works

Founded in 1996 by David and Liane Phillips, Cincinnati Works has become a model for similar programs in other places. After retiring early as managing director of a large accounting firm and then feeling a religious call to attack poverty in his hometown, Dave intensively researched and planned a program with his wife that they believed could move people from public assistance into work and self-sufficiency.

The Phillipses funded the initial stages themselves, then joined two other individual donors plus the Mathile Family Foundation, the Farmer Family Foundation, and the United Way of Greater Cincinnati in providing a three-year opening grant. Over the years, support from corporations like Western & Southern and JPMorgan Chase has also been important.

Cincinnati Works starts its "members" in a required class which teaches work ethics, problem-solving, personal budgeting, life values, self-confidence, employer expectations, and finally the techniques of applying and interviewing for jobs. Then the nonprofit offers intensive job-search and placement help. CW partners with over 70 employers in the area who open a wide range of job opportunities to graduates. The group makes around 600 job placements each year

After a member lands a job, CW staff continue to consult with both the worker and the employer for at least one year. Retaining a job, they emphasize, is almost as important as getting it in the first place. "One Job, One Year" and "Call Before You Quit" blare posters in the group's headquarters.

> Retaining a job, they emphasize, is almost as important as getting it in the first place. "One Job, One Year" and "Call Before You Quit" blare posters in the group's headquarters.

In addition to providing members with practical things like job training, child care, and transportation help, CW offers specialty services. Individuals with difficult backgrounds can get behavioral counseling, legal advocacy, mentoring, chaplain services, and anti-violence training. A study by the University of Cincinnati concluded that being a CW member reduced an individual's probability of felony indictment by almost 50 percent.

The final step in the CW process is advancement. Once a member has held the same job for a year, staffers create a plan to improve skills, education, or behavior such that the member can increase his or her earning power—with the goal being 200 percent of the poverty level, with health benefits. The average hourly pay of members is now two dollars higher than the state minimum wage.

And between 70 and 80 percent of Cincinnati Works members retain their job for at least a year. That is much better success than government job-training programs offer. Economist Diana Furchtgott-Roth notes that only 45 percent of graduates of the largest federal job-placement effort, the WIA Adult Program, manage to get and hold a job for more than six months. Only 20 percent of federal Job Corps graduates were employed after six months. Of all the individuals coming out of Cincinnati Works from 2005 to 2012, fully 84 percent are currently working.

In addition to boosting the jobless and underemployed, Cincinnati Works has been lauded by the *Harvard Business Review* for providing employers with a valuable source of stable entry-level workers—reducing the job turnover of some companies by half. And CW's services are provided entirely free to both individuals and employers. The privately funded nonprofit relies on 106 volunteers plus donors who cover the salaries of 27 employees. The program has been studied widely and replicated in Texas, Kentucky, Indiana, elsewhere in Ohio, and other places, with groups in more than a dozen other cities planning now to emulate its job-readiness services.

WorkFaith Connection

Some residents of Houston who were impressed by the results of Cincinnati Works offered to finance a similar organization in their city. With launch funding from Houston Endowment, the Fondren Foundation, the Looper Family Foundation, the YMCA of Greater Houston, and several smaller family foundations, plus a replication manual produced by the American Institute for Full Employment, WorkFaith Connection was created in 2007 with a faith-based approach to the life change that prepares the way for job readiness. The group collaborates with local homeless shelters and addiction centers to locate clients. It now has two locations in Houston and is scheduled to open a third in 2016.

"We're looking for people who have shifted from a heart of entitlement to a heart of gratitude," says WorkFaith Connection CEO Sandy Schultz. "It really doesn't matter what their past included. It matters where they are today. Once they make that switch, then that place of gratitude is what prepares them to receive guidance from us and to be good employees in the workplace."

Applicants first experience WorkFaith Connection through a two-and-a-half hour orientation meeting on Wednesdays. Their first official day of class is the following Friday, when they embark on an eight-day training camp that provides a toolkit for success, including skills in computers and finances, plus mentoring from a coach. The coursework provides a safe environment for workers-in-training to learn how to fall and then get back up.

Standards at WorkFaith Connection are high. Participants are expected to show up on time. They are given one pass for tardiness, but they have to explain to the class why they were late. "It's much easier to take your medicine at WorkFaith Connection and learn those lessons now than to lose a job," Schultz notes.

After completing the boot camp, WorkFaith Connection works with applicants on job placement and retention. The organization partners with many companies, typically in the range of 50 to 150 employees. Hiring managers at the partner firms say WFC graduates arrive with positive attitudes, and often high resilience, because they have learned to overcome serious obstacles in their lives. Houston's strong local economy provides steady demand for the services of WFC. The organization also enjoys solid support from local churches and donors.

Ralph Marek, co-owner of the Houston-based residential and commercial construction company Marek Brothers, has been a solid supporter of WorkFaith Connection for years. When he and his two siblings founded their company decades ago they made a pledge: if each managed to achieve a net worth of $1 million, they would create a foundation specifically geared toward lifting the poor out of poverty through employment. Today, the Marek Family Foundation fulfills that vision through $1.5 million in annual giving.

Marek sees WorkFaith Connection as an ideal combination of Christian service and economic sense. "Our family roots are in being poor, so we formed our foundation to help the poor, and the way you help the poor is by getting them employed," Marek says. Through the end of 2015, the Marek Family Foundation has invested about a million dollars in WorkFaith Connection, in steadily increasing grants.

Others like investment-company partner Robert Zorich support WFC by hiring graduates of the program. Zorich is also a donor and member of the group's board of directors. His foundation made its first grant of $10,000 to in 2008 and has since committed another $630,000 through 2015.

In less than ten years, with an annual budget that is still less than a million and a half dollars per year, WorkFaith Connection has exerted a notable influence on a major U.S. city. Since its first class of graduates in 2007, WFC has made 3,322 job placements in Houston. The average starting wage of its graduates is nearly $12 per hour, with an expectation of reaching $15 to $17 per hour with health insurance benefits.

Cara Program

One of the pioneering dependency-to-work nonprofits in the country is Chicago's Cara Program. Founded in 1991 by IT entrepreneur and philanthropist Tom Owens, Cara's mission is to locate impoverished men and women who are motivated to change, and propel them into the world of success and self-sufficiency.

Owens was moved to create Cara when he discovered that none of the many job programs at Chicago homeless shelters were successful at paving the way to long-term work. At best, job placements would be stopgap measures, seldom lasting more than a year. There were no support networks to help new workers remain at work, and no longer-term paths to sustainable incomes.

"I realized that most of these people had the capability of returning to a full life. All it would take is a little bit of money and some connections in order to spur them into it," Owens says. "I thought it was a tragedy that human capital went to waste in such a terrible environment."

Owens began devising a strategy to change tragedy into triumph. He realized that attitudes must be changed while new skills are being learned. Those principles formed the basis of the organization that would become the Cara Program.

Today, Cara is serving hundreds of Chicago residents each year who would otherwise be unemployed. It runs on a weekly class schedule of career and life-skills training. A unique element of the program is that participants don't officially graduate until they have reached the one-year mark of their job placement.

To prepare strugglers for competitive jobs, Cara operates two entrepreneurial businesses of its own that allow participants to gain the skills and track record needed to enter the open job market. The first business, Cleanslate, is a neighborhood beautification program that focuses on litter abatement, landscaping, and snow removal in 20 communities across Chicago. The second, TCP Staffing, is a temp agency offering short-term workers for administrative tasks, customer service, custodial positions, and other jobs. Combined, these enterprises raise close to $3 million in annual revenue for the Cara Program and generate hundreds of temporary and transitional jobs.

In 2014, the organization placed 311 clients in permanent jobs and 377 clients in temporary or transitional jobs. At one year, these employees had an average job retention rate of 78 percent, and earned an average wage of $10.66 per hour, more than $2 per hour higher than the minimum wage in Illinois.

Since its launch, the Cara Program has shifted 3,000 workers into stable, long-term employment. The Owens Foundation continues to be a top supporter, along with the Weinberg Foundation, which most recently committed a 2013-2016 operating grant of $450,000.

Cara specializes in entry-level jobs, and this presents challenges according to CEO Maria Kim. "The criteria for an entry-level employee in 2014 is very different than it was even five years ago," she says. "We've had good fortune working with manufacturing firms for general labor positions in the past. But with the advancement of robotics within the manufacturing sector, those jobs no longer require big, burly guys (who might have had a checkered past) to move goods around. They require a junior engineer who can handle the robotics of the machine." Adapting to the changing landscape of entry-level work will require creativity on the part of charities and philanthropists in the future.

StepUp Ministry

Most of the initiatives that have succeeded at drawing struggling adults into the work force have been conceived and designed by business people. The next entity to be profiled, however, was created by a church. StepUp Ministry was built on the ideas of several members of White Memorial Presbyterian Church in downtown Raleigh, North Carolina, and funded from the church outreach budget. The organization officially incorporated as a 501(c)(3) nonprofit in 1989.

Originally, StepUp Ministry provided transitional housing for families who were homeless or at risk of becoming homeless. Eventually, that mission transformed into a jobs-training approach. In 2004, a major grant from the White Memorial Community Fund laid the foundation for StepUp's current two-pronged approach that combines job workshops and life training.

The program begins with a weeklong, 32-hour classroom instruction period where students learn the ins and outs of how to find and keep employment. The complementary life-skills instruction continues for a full year. It is designed to help workers maintain stability in their homes and in jobs, and emphasizes the long haul.

StepUp Ministry CEO Steve Swayne has a keen interest in analytics, accountability, and understanding the circumstances that pull adults into poverty. By using careful tracking mechanisms, his program is able to document participant progress from joblessness to employment and practical hope.

> The attitude we look for is "I don't just need food or transitional housing. I need to change what I'm doing so that everything improves."

"Our goal is to be transparent and accountable, and always show donors concrete, up-to-the-minute results," he says. "The nonprofit sector as a whole could benefit from placing more emphasis on the veracity and reliability of our results. Data ought to be the determining factor in the long-term planning of any organization."

StepUp's own results are impressive. With an operating budget of $1.4 million in 2013, the ministry made 363 job placements. Of that total, 57 percent were ex-offenders, 27 percent were homeless, and 25 percent had a history of substance abuse.

Sheldon Fox, owner of an accounting firm in Raleigh, first encountered StepUp Ministry as a volunteer. He helped strugglers create sustainable personal budgets and then make financial plans for the future. The satisfactions of that experience led Fox to provide substantial financial support, and then embark on a six-year tenure on the board of directors, including a stint as chairman.

"The program is very efficient and effective," says Fox. "StepUp has been committed to getting better and better over time." The ministry recently expanded to Greensboro, where it made 181 job placements in 2013, and is now seeking to bring its training to other parts of North Carolina.

Life Learning Center

As a successful real-estate developer, Bill Butler created more than 18 million square feet of office and retail space and managed 32 hotels across the U.S. But Butler is interested in far more than real estate. He also wants to improve his home community, and particularly to change the lives of its less fortunate residents by teaching self-sufficiency.

When Butler investigated existing social-service efforts he found that many offered short-term help but no permanent solutions to poverty. "I wanted to find a constructive pathway to change, sustainability, dignity, and contribution," he says. He sought solutions with the same methodical determination that drives his real estate ventures, and in 2006 created what he called the Life Learning Center in his home region of northern Kentucky, across the Ohio River from Cincinnati.

"The Life Learning Center is for the person who is ready to do something drastically different in all aspects of life," Butler says. "The attitude we look for is 'I don't just need food or transitional housing. I need to change what I'm doing so that everything improves.' The center strengthens individuals so they are ready for real and lasting change, and we only admit candidates who are willing and able to commit."

Applicants begin the process with a one-hour interview and assessment that includes a drug screening. After gaining admission, individuals go through an introductory class on Wednesday, and then are enrolled in a series of seminars that provide guidance on building productive habits and character traits, good relations with other people, healthy patterns at home, and so forth. Each participant also works one-on-one with a life coach during this time. Job-skills classes are taken in parallel. And the training culminates in a job-placement search.

The entire curriculum is 16 weeks. Two thirds of participants are employed by the time they finish the program, and most hold onto their new posts for at least a year. The nonprofit accepts no government funds, relying entirely on private support. In 2015, the organization moved into a spectacular new headquarters in a restored foundry. The renovated building offers a mix of classroom space, lecture halls, library, computer lab, training rooms, childcare facilities, a cafeteria, and a fitness center.

STRIVE

Put together two Manhattan banker/donors disturbed by a chronic lack of employment among many inner-city residents, and an East Harlem ex-convict and drug addict who got clean and then earned a master's degree from Columbia University. The result? An unusual job-training program built on (very) tough love. It's called STRIVE, and it has proven effective among economically struggling populations.

One third of STRIVE clients are former prisoners, about a third have no high-school diploma or GED. Yet two thirds of its graduates are placed in jobs, at pay averaging 150 percent of their state minimum wage. And more than 70 percent of these workers stick in their new employment. Meanwhile the average cost per job placement for STRIVE is less than $2,000.

As with the other private job programs profiled in this chapter, these outcomes completely eclipse results from typical government-run job programs. The U.S. Department of Labor's Job Corps program, which serves similar persons, costs almost eight times as much per participant, even though only a fifth of its alums are employed after six months.

One big difference, Manhattan Institute scholar Kay Hymowitz has noted, is that STRIVE builds "the all-important 'soft skills'"—respect, punctuality, initiative, honesty, reliability—in a determinedly no-nonsense way. Uncooperative attitudes and excuses for failure are broken down by the STRIVE instructors, all of whom are themselves people who have triumphed over corrosive street habits. The result of their strict demands, in-your-face intensity, and follow-up and support (graduates are monitored for at least two years after graduation and assisted as needed) is creation in the participant of a new "understanding of the manners and values of an alien mainstream work world."

STRIVE's successes have allowed it to spread to more than two dozen cities. About 50,000 difficult clients have been trained under its auspices, a number that rises every year. Since its founding, STRIVE has enjoyed philanthropic support from a range of donors like the Clark, Abell, and Annie E. Casey foundations. The Harry and Jeanette Weinberg Foundation has been a stalwart backer from early on. And current donors include Walmart, the Blackstone Group, and the Rudin Foundation. Each chapter is mostly funded by local philanthropists.

America Works

Labor experts will tell you that the biggest general difference between government job-training programs and nonprofit counterparts is that the privately run efforts put a much heavier emphasis on actually getting a job—any job—and holding it. Government programs offer lots of incentives for course-taking, school enrollment, and credential punching, but rarely demand that the participant go into the job market and actually take a position. The private programs, on the other hand, have found that real work of any sort usually leads to more and better work in the future. The fact that good non-government efforts turn roughly twice as large a fraction of their participants into long-term workers suggests they are right about this.

That said, it is nonetheless true that all of the programs profiled above still rely on various form of instruction and social training of enrollees before they introduce them into the job market. There is a viewpoint, however, that even this training is much less important than just going to work and then learning on the job. Call this the "work first, train later" philosophy.

America Works is a nonprofit founded in 1984 that now operates in nine states across the nation. The America Works program involves just two to four weeks of job-readiness training, and matching of participants to actual jobs begins very early. Within a month in most cases the candidate has been placed in a job and expected to show up. Once work has begun, training, classes, mental health services, and so forth sometimes continue, but work gets priority.

The group's literature explains what it calls "The Work First Theory," engrained in the organization by founder Peter Cove.:

> America Works believes that work should be the central focus in social policy. This is why we work to place clients into jobs rapidly. Gaining employment is the surest path to independence because work socializes and integrates those who are disadvantaged.... The clients' success in the workplace will make them more successful in the classroom, leading to a better and independent life.

Rather than building elaborate preparation processes into its operating procedures, America Works focuses on the outcome of getting a person to work as soon as possible.

America Works partners with a large network of employers who are seeking customer service reps, health-care aides, drivers, security guards, maintenance workers, receptionists, data-entry specialists, food preparers, machinery operators, and similar jobs. AW matches the hard-to-employ individuals who enter its doors, most often coming from government welfare or social-service agencies, with these often-hard-to-fill jobs. The nonprofit doesn't get paid unless its candidate succeeds in the position for an agreed period—typically 3-6 months. So it is entirely a performance-based model.

America Works has found jobs for 300,000 individuals since its beginning, many of them long-term welfare recipients, people living in shelters, released prisoners, young people aging out of foster care, and so forth. The nonprofit has carved a deep niche for itself in "performance-based" contracting with government agencies. This means it only gets paid if the hard-to-place job seeker sent by the government agency actually gets a job and then holds it for an agreed period. Studies have given the group high ratings for getting workers with these backgrounds to hold jobs for at least six months. One New York State Department of Labor examination found that 88 percent of people placed by this "work first" nonprofit remained off the welfare rolls three years later.

A driving obstacle: What to do about transportation

A prerequisite for securing and maintaining a job is a reliable means of getting to work on a timely basis. Yet economic strugglers often lack transportation options. Poor persons who lack cars or access to good public transportation can face serious barriers to long-term work.

A 2011 study from the Brookings Institution found that 7.5 million households in major metropolitan areas had no access to a privately owned vehicle. A majority of these people were lower income. Among all low-income households, roughly one-in-four have no car.

> The federal Job Corps program costs almost eight times as much per person, even though only a fifth of its participants are employed after six months.

While vehicle-less households tend to cluster near public-transit corridors, many still face challenges in reaching jobs efficiently. Several worthy nonprofits are working to overcome this problem. Vehicles for Change, which serves the Maryland-Virginia-Washington, D.C. region, solicits donations of used cars, and then rehabs the vehicles into viable options for the working poor. The Milwaukee-based Ways to Work takes a financing approach: the nonprofit provides low-cost loans to the poor in order to make car ownership feasible. The Lift Garage is a relatively new nonprofit that offers low-cost car repair. A valuable side-effect of this service is that the group is able to simultaneously train previously unskilled persons in the field of auto mechanics.

Another way donors prevent transportation problems from blocking workforce development is to be sure their organizations are located near transit hubs. WorkFaith Connection, for instance, consciously located their offices adjacent to a major bus stop. After a good experience using transit to become trained for work, it is easier for graduates to master the connections needed to get to actual jobs.

REDF helps strugglers by creating businesses

Some of the finest programs for helping people with poor work histories transition into successful employment have taken a more direct route: They create sheltered businesses where strugglers can master the necessary skills right on the job, while earning some pay, and creating value that helps fund the overall program. Their central premise is that work (rather than social work) is the best anti-poverty strategy.

A pioneer in this area was the Roberts Enterprise Development Fund, now known merely by the initials REDF. Founded in 1997 in the Bay Area of California, it was a philanthropic innovation of George Roberts and his wife, as their contribution against burgeoning homelessness in their region. They felt that an employment-centered, business-building solution would be much more effective than just offering handouts. And as one of the country's top venture capitalists (co-founder of Kohlberg Kravis Roberts & Co.), Roberts knew something about how to create new enterprises. The sector REDF helped invent is sometimes referred to as venture philanthropy.

At first, REDF gave grants to existing nonprofits that tried to help homeless people get jobs. Seeking better outcomes, Roberts decided to start offering "equity-like grants and business assistance" that would create freestanding small businesses where "people facing the greatest barriers to work"—those living on the street, convicts, school dropouts, the mentally ill, alcoholics, etc., who would otherwise depend on hand-to-mouth charity or government assistance—can get a foot on the employment ladder.

The entities REDF funds are expected to be business-like in their operations, paying careful attention to efficiency while offering useful services or products that will generate revenue streams that can be reinvested into training their employees. The businesses—sometimes called social enterprises—aren't intended to make significant profits; indeed most lose money. Success is not measured by REDF solely through financial returns, though, but also in terms of human progress and improved behavioral patterns.

Today it is not unusual for successful business people to orient their philanthropy toward market-based solutions to social problems. Roberts was early to the party. When he gave a million dollars to one social enterprise so it could set up a cabinetmaking shop where minorities could be trained, he insisted the organization take out a bank loan to cover the other half of the project's costs—because the pressure of their commitment to the bank would keep them focused on running the operation like entrepreneurs rather than like a giveaway.

Ultimately, Roberts told us in an interview, "We're trying to get people into some kind of a job, rather than sitting idly. The expectation is that they can eventually move from the nonprofit sector to a more mainstream job. Success is regular work with health insurance and enough money to have an independent place to live. That is what we shoot for."

"The premise here is that work should be available to everyone, everywhere," says Carla Javits, who has served as REDF's executive director since 2007. "If people want to work and are able, we should find a way for them to work." Here are examples of some social enterprises that have recently been supported by REDF:

- Chrysalis runs a maintenance and property-management service for buildings in the Skid Row section of Los Angeles, as well as street-cleaning crews who contract with merchants in the Fashion District.
- Community Housing Partnership has a growing business providing lobby services to landlords in San Francisco.
- 360 Solutions provides pest-control in southern California.
- The Center for Employment Opportunities has maintenance contracts that keep its workers busy in Oakland and San Diego.

Mathematica Policy Research recently studied seven of REDF's social enterprises and their alumni. In the year before their sheltered work experience, only 39 percent of participants had managed to work for six continuous months. In the year after their REDF experience, however, fully 67 percent worked for at least six continuous months. Not surprisingly, their housing situation was consequently more stable. The total income of participants didn't change, but they drew less on government transfers and relied more on their own earnings.

In 2004, REDF converted itself from a family foundation into an independent nonprofit. The aim was to attract funding from other philanthropists that would allow the group to expand its footprint and methods. That happened, with grants coming from partners like the Woodcock, Kresge, Weingart, and Kellogg foundations. REDF also formed working alliances and offered assistance to other nonprofits and venture philanthropies, including New Door Ventures, Juma Ventures, and the Women's Bean Project.

Since its formation, REDF has supported 50 social enterprises that have employed more than 8,700 people with little previous success in the workforce. These individuals have earned more than $140 million, and 70 percent still held their jobs a year after starting. Workers in REDF-supported social ventures saw an 85 percent decrease in their reliance on government assistance. REDF's goal is to help create an additional 2,500 jobs in the near future by expanding beyond the eight counties it currently operates in (half in the Bay Area, half in greater Los Angeles).

Roberts says the REDF model could be replicated in other areas of the country as well. "There is no reason the 25 largest cities in the country can't apply this," he states. "We'd be happy to help. Let's assume each of those 25 cities have 1,000 people a year go through their programs. That's a quarter of a million of our poorest people redirected in 10 years. Individual donors can make a meaningful change."

Faith-based mentoring from Jobs for Life

Workforce development can be delivered with a faith-based component. This offers two advantages. One is that the faith element is often helpful at getting at deeper issues of missing self-respect or confidence or accountability that often interfere with work. Another advantage is that local churches can supply funds, volunteers, and space necessary to get started.

Jobs for Life is an umbrella group for a network of churches and nonprofit organizations that break down work barriers (as well as racial barriers) all across the country. It began in Raleigh, North Carolina, in the late 1990s when an African-American pastor who needed his parking lot paved formed a friendship with a white contractor. The two began meeting weekly for lunch, and soon discovered overlapping problems: the contractor had trucks sitting idle due to lack of drivers, while the pastor had many unemployed men in his community. That led to the idea of forming an alliance between businesses and churches, and JFL was born.

Today, the Jobs for Life curriculum is available in 275 cities. It is a 16-week course that pairs participants with a one-on-one mentor. Each class provides two hours of instruction in soft skills, discussion of the importance of work in daily life, and exercises in character development. A significant benefit of JFL is the low cost per-person served—$188 in 2013—thanks to its church-sponsored and volunteer structure.

"We have designed it so that the financial requirement is minimal," says Daniel Alexander, the group's regional director for the southeast. "The time and relationship investments are bigger—which we believe is the right emphasis, because the personal touch is how people find hope and jobs."

JFL is a rare effort to draw on the largely untapped potential of the local church to transform the lives of the jobless. "We have this huge opportunity to mobilize the church—this extraordinary resource—that's been just giving stuff away," says David Spickard, CEO of Jobs for Life. "We've all been in the welfare mentality to outsource the poor to other programs, instead of creating a relationship-based helping network."

Of America's 460,000 churches, 62 percent give away food, but only 2 percent encourage work as a more permanent, effective, and dignified means of alleviating poverty.

To underscore his point, Spickard points to statistics showing that of America's 460,000 churches, 62 percent give away food, but only 2 percent encourage work as a more permanent, effective, and dignified means of alleviating poverty. Jobs for Life is working to "flip the list" and put work first. Most of the grunt duties in its model can be carried out by local churches, leading Spickard to call the program "a church-equipping" ministry.

Churches pay to join the network and can then access the teaching materials through an online portal. Jobs for Life takes a localist approach. Pastors and volunteer businessmen on the ground are given wide leeway to adjust the curriculum from Raleigh to the needs and peculiarities of their own city.

As a Christian organization, Jobs for Life seeks to strengthen the character of participants at the same time it is offering practical skills. "It's their identity that really needs to be addressed," says Spickard. "It's about character and it's about community."

About 20 percent of JFL's revenue comes from fees paid for its curriculum; the other 80 percent of its national budget comes from philanthropic supporters, including the Cary Oil Foundation, the Kharis Foundation, and Nashville's Memorial Foundation.

More faith-based training: Belay Enterprises

Belay Enterprises was launched in Denver in 1995 in the hope of financing microenterprises in the same way that small loans to local entrepreneurs have been used to spur economic activity in developing countries. The founders quickly discovered, however, that microfinancing wasn't as effective in the U.S. as abroad, partly because their dollars didn't stretch nearly as far. So the organization transitioned to a different model: incubating businesses as a way of helping hard-to-reach members of their community get jobs.

Bud's Warehouse was the first incubated business of Belay Enterprises. It offers, in a 20,000 square foot building, a variety of new, used, and antique home improvement supplies. All of the electrical fixtures, lumber, windows, and so forth are donated. Bud's employs men coming out of prison, or addiction, or homelessness, to clean, sort, refurbish, and stock materials, which are then sold to the public at around half of retail prices.

In addition to Bud's Warehouse, Belay Enterprises has founded and incubated five other social enterprises during its two decades of operation. Baby Bud's is a thrift store specializing in infant supplies. Freedom Cleaning provides commercial services to local churches and businesses. Good Neighbor Garage is a car recycling program. New Beginnings is a custom woodworking shop. Purple Door Coffee employs as servers youths who have been homeless. Each firm is incorporated as its own LLC.

Belay Enterprises was created by an evangelical Christian nonprofit called Mile High Ministries. Its largest initial funders were Cherry Hills Community Church, the United Way, the Tocqueville Society, the Anschutz Foundation, and the Adolph Coors Foundation. Five years into its operations, Belay Enterprises was financially stable thanks to revenue generated by the businesses it created. Belay relies on philanthropy to help cover the startup costs of new ventures until they are operating stably, but then they are expected to be self-supporting.

"We love going to donors and telling them that they're basically making an investment in the organization," says director James Reiner, "and that we won't be returning to them year after year asking them to sustain a business. We're aiming toward getting 80 percent to 90 percent of our budget covered by revenue."

Belay Enterprises uses faith to build cohesion, effort, and responsibility among employees of its enterprises. Each Wednesday morning at Bud's Warehouse, for example, staff members convene for a morning "hood check." Everyone around the table shares developments in their lives, and asks for prayer. Employees hold one another accountable.

"We're an operation built on second chances," Reiner says. "Grace and forgiveness permeate this place. When people experience that, they want their lives to change too. Most of our people have not had positive relationships or had people care about them, so this new community at work is a huge propeller to success. Helping people develop their faith allows them to see that there are bigger things than their problems."

For soft skills, Reiner has found that the best training is on-the-job. "We give classes on anger management, for instance. But it's best when they actually struggle with a conflict situation on the floor and we can walk them through that and help them learn from it," he says.

Belay Enterprises aims to have new entrants complete all of its programs, work at one of their incubated businesses for more than one month, and use that experience to graduate to a market job in the community. They achieve this with between 30 and 45 percent of the individuals who come to them for help.

Christian commerce in Milwaukee

A similar faith-based model is employed at an organization launched around the same time as Bud's, but in Milwaukee. The Community Warehouse feels like a neighborhood home improvement store. Beneath the surface, though, it's a nonprofit that changes lives.

Community Warehouse was launched in 2002 to provide low-income people with affordable building materials. Contractors, retailers, distributors, manufacturers, and other businesses donate their unused building supplies to the group. It then sells them for about a quarter of the regular retail value.

The Community Warehouse hires "second-chance" workers—men and women who have had troubling holding work in the past. They sort, price, and display the donated goods in neat rows, help customers on the shop floor, and work the cash registers. Eight years after creating this successful jobs program, the nonprofit established its Milwaukee Working division to create even more full-time opportunities where job-challenged men and women could experience the dignity of work.

Milwaukee Working trains and mentors workers who deliver a variety of services to for-profit businesses. These include tasks like pick-pack-and-ship, sorting operations, and electronics disassembly for recycling. One of its most successful ventures is Milwaukee Working Marketplace, which sells used items—mostly books, DVDs, and small power tools—on Amazon.

In its woodshop, MW assembles home-improvement products for sale at Community Warehouse: bathroom vanities, kitchen cabinets, pre-hung doors. It disassembles old basketball courts and wood floors, repurposing the lumber for reuse and resale. Its building disassembly crew extracts recyclable materials from old structures prior to demolition, again to repurpose them. It collect unwanted pallets from local businesses, repairs them, and sell them to customers throughout the Milwaukee market.

Sales revenues from these enterprises provide wages for the workers while they learn skills in carpentry, computers, customer service, and logistics. The Community Warehouse and Milwaukee Working provide large doses of Christian support and love to participants as they train. And they draw them into the mainstream commercial work.

Alicia Manning at the Lynde and Harry Bradley Foundation comments that "we support these groups because they help people build the capacity to work, support their families, and become part of the broader economy." Along with Bradley, about 50 other companies, religious organizations, and foundations, plus 75 or so individual donors, help defray the administrative costs of the nonprofit.

Sector-specific training: BioTechnical Institute

Another model that donors might consider is one that trains the disadvantaged to fill gaps in specific sectors of the economy. Health care is a top example. Today there are shortages in many places of health attendants of various sorts, and the U.S. Bureau of Labor Statistics estimates that an additional 5 million jobs will open in health and social-service occupations between 2012 and 2022. Linking Americans currently disconnected from the workforce with these jobs begging to be filled could yield a double success.

The nonprofit BioTechnical Institute of Maryland is doing just that in Baltimore—a city with a poverty rate of 25 percent. Dr. Margaret Penno, then a researcher at Johns Hopkins University, founded the organization in 1998. She had firsthand experience with the problem of high turnover in entry-level biotechnology jobs. Training individuals who lack a college degree but have the ability to learn necessary skills seemed the natural solution.

"The biotech industry in Baltimore was growing and they needed good people," says BTI director Kathleen Weiss. "The economic argument was that non-degreed individuals are going to stay longer. And you don't necessarily have to pay them as much as a college graduate."

BTI started with one program to train lab associates—a nine-week curriculum of lectures and hands-on exercises. Staff soon discovered that a pre-training program was needed to refresh the math and technical skills of applicants. With critical support from the Annie E. Casey Foundation and East Baltimore Development Inc., BTI launched BioSTART, a 10-week program that offers basic technical background, training in professionalism, and essential skills for the lab.

What we try to instill in people is that they are now professionals. When they put that lab coat on, they are putting that professionalism on.

We had an opportunity to visit BTI's training facility. Thanks to philanthropic support, it has a major asset on site: a full-scale laboratory with all the requisite equipment and a staff of trained biotechnologists. After successfully completing BioSTART, participants are placed in a 100-hour internship in this working lab. BTI covers the cost of the internship. Participating employers often end up hiring the lab's interns.

BTI's average applicant is an African-American woman in her 30s who is a single mother. "People come in our doors with a lot of baggage: often unemployed or under-employed," Weiss says. "Their self-esteem may not be so good. So what we try to instill in people in the pre-training is that they are now professionals. When they put that lab coat on, they are putting that professionalism on. And it's transformative."

Applicants must have at least a high-school diploma. After they graduate from BTI, they are eligible for 6 credits toward an associate degree in biotechnology from Baltimore City Community College. To date, BTI has produced 322 graduates, who have enjoyed a job placement rate of 76 percent. Their average starting salary is $25,000.

In addition to philanthropic support, BTI has an earned-revenue component through a social venture known as BioSciConcepts. The BTI staff offer fee-based workshops geared toward professionals in the technology world. Topics are wide ranging and include an introduction to cell culture and an exploration of molecular biology. Revenue generated from BioSciConcepts helps fund BTI's programs to equip struggling workers for job success.

Critical early support for BTI came from the Baltimore-based Abell Foundation, which funds workforce development as one of its core areas. Other mainstay supporters include the Charles Bauer, Casey, Weinberg, and Wells Fargo foundations.

Other sector-specific job feeders also operate in Baltimore. The Baltimore Alliance for Careers in Healthcare, for instance, seeks to channel at-risk workers into short-staffed health-care occupations in the area. Similar nonprofits that train disadvantaged workers while simultaneously helping solve labor-market imbalances in their home areas also exist in other cities. There is room for much philanthropic invention on this front.

Supporting business growth in poor neighborhoods

Encouraging the success of businesses in troubled communities is another way philanthropists can boost the hard-to-employ. Two examples of philanthropic aggregators that help donors fulfill that vision in different regions are Pacific Community Ventures and Rising Tide Capital.

Pacific Community Ventures was created by former Silicon Valley executives wanting to invest in business creation in poor communities. PCV's services include various forms of "advice and capital to help small businesses succeed." Specifically, they advise potential founders of small businesses, provide loans, share information on best practices, and evaluate financials.

"I co-founded PCV in 1998 when I realized that small businesses could transform communities if they had the same advice and capital that was being made available to venture-backed technology startups," states entrepreneur Bud Colligan. In 2013, PCV connected 256 small firms across 11 states with expertise from its lineup of advisers. The total number of jobs in PCV companies rose 22 percent that same year.

A similar model exists on the East Coast. Rising Tide Capital is based in Jersey City, New Jersey. It is built on the notion that neighborhood revitalization begins from within—by tapping into the entrepreneurial talent and ambition that already exists in the community.

RTC provides budding local entrepreneurs in lower-income districts with three types of capital: financial, social, and knowledge. The help is delivered through two primary programs. The Community Business Academy is a 12-week course held on Saturdays and weeknights after the workday has ended. Its coursework, offered twice per year, trains participants in the basic principles of business management.

The second program, called Business Acceleration Services, provides more focused one-on-one training and seminars for those seeking to open a new business or expand an existing one. RTC's typical entrepreneur is a 40-year-old mother of two children, a minority, with a household income of less than $35,000.

By investing in entrepreneurs, RTC believes it reaps several layers of good results: A better life for the entrepreneur. Jobs for others in the community. And new enterprises that bring services or products the neighborhood was missing. Entrepreneurial philanthropists could extend these benefits to new places by building on these examples.

Common traits of outstanding work programs

We can identify some common traits in the effective work-bolstering charities described in this chapter. Here are eight:

1. Focus on participants anxious to change their lives

People firmly set in a dependence mindset or in self-destructive behaviors will rarely be changed even by the best programs. There are plenty of strugglers hungry for dramatic change in their lives; find them and assist them in making the hard adjustments.

"We can help someone get a job who wants a job, regardless of their past. But we can't make somebody want a job," says Sandy Schultz of WorkFaith Connection. "If someone doesn't want to be here and doesn't want employment, there is little we can do for them."

2. Offer practical training that fills a marketplace need

Training must prepare workers for actual jobs that are unfilled locally today, not imaginary future jobs. "The Achilles' heel in workforce development has been insufficient focus on preparing people for real, existing work in our employer community, and sometimes a failure to be sure people are ready for those jobs" says Carla Javits of REDF.

3. Always think about what employers need

The most successful organizations keep an ear cocked for what employers want. Improving an employer's bottom line via productive workers, reduced training costs, and reduced turnover will bring job-offering companies flocking; they can't hire strictly out of charity.

"Effective employment programs are like brokers," explains Donn Weinberg of the Weinberg Foundation. "Employers can't find enough good people on their own, and they come to trust these programs to deliver a flow of reliable candidates. The reputation of the employment program is based on making sure that their training is relevant and works."

4. Emphasize job retention and advancement

Employment-challenged populations—high-school dropouts, single mothers, minorities, etc.—experience significantly less job stability, retention, and movement up the ladder than other groups. Adroit training groups realize the gravity of this. They make job placements but don't stop there—showing workers how to hold onto work, scout opportunities for advancement, and prepare themselves to step up.

"For many folks, it's not just about getting a job. It's about keeping a job over the long term," says Maria Kim of Cara. Incentives to ensure that graduates of workforce programs stay in touch are useful in this regard. The Women's Bean Project—a social enterprise based in Denver—pays its graduates $50 to check in every six months. Today, the organization's alumni follow-up rate is 80 percent, compared to an abysmal 20 percent when they simply said "please" without the financial enticement.

5. Recognize spiritual and psychological needs

Work involves a lot more than economics, particularly among struggling populations. One of the many reasons private nonprofits are better mechanisms for pulling disconnected persons into the workforce is because they have greater freedom than government entities to work with the whole human—including spiritual, moral, and psychological dimensions, self-image, and character development. Agencies of the state cannot push people in these areas, but voluntary groups, varying to reflect the range of human needs, can pull levers that would be inappropriate for a government agency. They can apply insights of responsibility, right conduct, personal value, religious faith, and the like. The result: changed hearts, changed minds, changed behavior, changed outlooks on life.

6. Provide missing community and social structure

A community that supports strivers, that elevates hard work and success, that redirects failure, can make all the difference. Job strugglers often have fewer people and networks in their life they can fall back on. Nonprofit programs that offer consistent tough love can help in this area.

7. Try to find models that earn your group revenue

Although not mandatory for success, a model that brings in revenue will make a program much more sustainable and expandable. Donors are attracted to nonprofits that have earnings, not only because that makes them stronger financially but because it is a market signal that their product is valued by customers willing to pay for it.

8. Operating businesses can be helpful

There are benefits beyond the cash flow in operating a revenue-generating business under the nonprofit infrastructure. These ventures give strugglers a safe place to learn work skills, providing a valuable track record of employment that can then be taken to the next job opportunity. And they become laboratories where charities learn what really works and what doesn't.

Reaching Disconnected Young People

When young people fail to connect to the workforce, severe economic and social problems frequently follow for both those individuals and the larger society they are part of. Alienated from legitimate jobs, these youths will turn to illegal activities, a government-subsidized life, or unproductive dependence on others. Despair and unrest will often follow.

There are millions of young Americans in the "disconnected" category: teenage parents, high-school dropouts, graduates who are not employed or continuing their education, the grossly underemployed. A Brookings Institution analysis published in 2014 described a "lost decade" for youth employment:

- The sharpest declines in U.S. employment between 2000 and 2011 fell among teens and young adults.
- The share of teens with any paid employment during the year dropped from 55 percent in 2000 to 28 percent in 2011.
- The share of young adults with any paid employment during the year dropped from 82 percent in 2000 to 69 percent in 2011.

Not surprisingly, Brookings found that more vulnerable populations were disproportionately hit by these employment declines. Young people with less education and less work experience were particularly battered by the depressed job market of the past decade. Experts say the factors listed below are particularly likely to depress job success among new entrants to the work force; good training programs must recognize and overcome them:

1. Growing up in a fractured family
Family breakdown brings greater instability, less income, and less adult attention into children's lives. Today's soaring rates of single-parenting are putting many children at a disadvantage.

2. A lack of successful role models
Many urban minority youths see relatively few successes in the population around them. "A lot of the students we work with are feeling on the outside," says Eshauna Smith, president of the Urban Alliance, which specializes in connecting African-American and Latino youths to constructive work.

3. No track record
For young people who fail to graduate from high school, or who graduate but lack work experience, the résumé can be unnaturally thin.

4. Disconnected from practical vocational training
The contemporary emphasis on going to college has eclipsed good vocational training that might be more relevant to some youthful strugglers. Even where programs exist, there can be obstacles that prevent young people from finding or seizing them.

5. Homeless

Around 380,000 minors experience a homeless episode longer than a week in a given year. That can interfere with efforts to hold a job. (Some organizations have cropped up to address this problem specifically, like Juma Ventures of San Francisco, which places homeless youngsters in positions its creates in its own ventures. The successful nonprofit has expanded to Oakland and San Diego, as well as Washington State and Louisiana.)

6. Drug abuse

Nearly a quarter of high-school seniors used marijuana during the past month, according to data from the National Institute on Drug Abuse, and prescription drugs are now abused by 15 percent of high-school seniors. Drug abuse can change personal incentives, interfere with education, alter brain behaviors, eliminate drug-tested jobs, and otherwise become a sizable employment barrier.

7. Criminal activity

Although incarceration rates for individuals under the age of 21 have declined in recent years, law enforcement agencies currently make about 1.5 million arrests of minors annually; 86 percent of these are males—substantial minorities of whom have damaged their employment prospects via a criminal history. (More on this in Chapter 6.)

8. Unwed pregnancy

The CDC reports that 305,388 babies were born to mothers between the ages of 15 and 19 in 2012. These girls often drop out of school and go on welfare assistance, a dead-end that can make it hard to return to mainstream employment.

Not every factor influencing at-risk kids works to their disadvantage. Duncan Campbell, founder of the youth-mentorship organization Friends of the Children, has found that troubled youths often have a significant capacity for entrepreneurship, perhaps because they have spent so much time relying on themselves (which will either break a child or make him unusually independent and resourceful). Campbell and other donors like Gerald Chertavian, founder of the youth job-development group Year Up, have been able to identify resilience, capacity for risk-taking, tenacity, and a go-getter attitude as strengths of a subset of disadvantaged youth—who some practitioners refer to, for those very reasons, as "opportunity youth."

Chertavian encourages participants in his program to view their struggles as potential assets rather than automatic deficits. "We see the challenges and barriers that they've faced as what has made them strong and built up their grit," he told us. "We take a strength-based perspective rather than a problem perspective. That's fundamentally important. That which you have faced and endured in the past can make you a better employee, rather than someone who is damaged." Character training can be crucial in helping young people internalize, and act on, this distinction.

The role of education
Many young people are out of the workforce for a very good reason: they are busy in school, earning credentials that eventually will make them better candidates in the labor market. Youths from troubled backgrounds, however, are more likely to be disconnected from school, or struggling in high school or college. There is positive news on high-school dropouts: between 1990 and 2010, the national dropout rate declined from 12 percent to 7 percent. Alas, the remaining dropouts tend to be tightly clustered in urban schools, known as "dropout factories," which disproportionately include poor and minority students.

> Only 45 percent of graduates of the largest federal job-placement effort manage to get and hold a job for at least six months. The successful charitable programs do about twice as well.

For students who do graduate from high school, around two thirds enroll in college of some sort. But many more of these students than is widely understood will fail to finish their degree. Barely half of first-time, full-time undergraduates pursuing a bachelor's degree finish within six years at the same university. And completion rates are dismally lower at community colleges, especially for low-income students. Just 13 percent of students in the lowest income quartile who started a two-year degree in the 2003-2004 school year completed it by 2009, according to data from the National Center for Education Statistics.

February 2014 data from the Pew Research Center found that millennials (ages 25-32 as this book is written) who had a bachelor's degree or more exhibited an unemployment rate of just 3.8 percent, while millennials with only a high-school diploma were unemployed at 12.2 percent. Fully 22 percent of millennials with only a high-school degree were very low income.

Donors in search of practical solutions to the problem of young people who are disconnected from the workforce mustn't see college education as the only answer, because there are many young people who will never cross that line. Rather, the goal should be to encourage the acquisition of skills and knowledge demanded by the marketplace. As Tamar Jacoby, president of Opportunity America, notes, there are good avenues outside of universities.

"Americans have a host of postsecondary options other than a four-year degree—associate degrees, occupational certificates, industry certifications, apprenticeships," she says. "Many economists are bullish about the prospects of what they call 'middle-skilled' workers. In coming years, according to some, at least a third and perhaps closer to half of all U.S. jobs will require more than high school but less than four years of college—and most will involve some sort of technical or practical training."

Nonprofits like Year Up focus on linking disadvantaged young people with these types of "middle-skill" jobs. Suzanne Klahr, founder of the entrepreneurship-training organization BUILD that is geared toward high-schoolers, says "the only way that we will change this vicious cycle of poverty is by making sure that young people are prepared for the world of work in the twenty-first century. For some students, it's trade school. For some students, it's community college. For some, it's four years plus graduate school."

The authors of a 2011 study from the Harvard University Graduate School of Education caution against focusing too narrowly on a single definition of educational success. "It is time to widen our lens and build a more finely articulated pathways system," they argue. Practical economic skills can be as valuable to young people as liberal-arts education.

The Jenesis Group is a family foundation based in Dallas that is acutely interested in connecting disadvantaged youths with jobs in need of filling. It was established in 1987 by Ron Jenson, who was very successful in the telecommunications and health-insurance fields. More than formal education, his foundation's preferred mechanism is to use social enterprises to firmly connect at-risk teens and early adults with the working world.

"The market is telling us loud and clear that a skill gap exists out there," says Kim Tanner, senior program officer with Jenesis. "One of the most critical barriers to entry in the workforce is soft skills and professional skills that aren't easily taught in the classroom. You really need hands-on experience to gain some kinds of understanding." And so her foundation has made significant long-term commitments to Year Up and Genesys Works, two practical charities profiled later in this chapter that focus on giving young people real-world job experience while still in high school.

Another funder that has been influential in this area is the Annie E. Casey Foundation. Casey is a major supporter of innovative organizations like Girls Who Code, a nonprofit with locations in New York, Detroit, San Francisco, and San Jose that shepherds underrepresented women into careers in computer science. Casey has also been crucial in funding research on youth unemployment. In a recent report subtitled "Restoring Teen and Young Adult Connections to Opportunity," the foundation concluded:

> In the end, work itself is the strongest and most effective "program." Early job experience increases the likelihood of more work in the future, as well as more employer-sponsored education. A continuum of work experiences from the teen years onward—including volunteer and community service, summer and part-time jobs, work-study experiences, internships and apprenticeships—build job-readiness skills, knowledge and confidence. These encompass not just workplace and financial skills, but also the broader "soft skills" of taking responsibility and initiative, working in teams, focusing on problem-solving, and learning how to contribute.

Connecting high-schoolers to real jobs: Genesys Works

It's easy to mistake the Genesys Works offices—located on the 39th floor of the KBR tower in downtown Houston—for the well-appointed workspace of a Fortune 500 company. A glass-paneled front door gives way to a reception area, then cubicles on the left and offices on the right that hum with activity.

Inside two large meeting rooms at the opposite end of the office suite, young people are assembled in semi-circles. Some are taking professional skills classes—how to interact with a supervisor, how to dress appropriately, how to build confidence—while others are immersed in technical training. From their appearances it would be easy to mistake these high-school students as products of middle-class families. In fact, they all come from at-risk backgrounds.

"We exist to change the trajectory of life for low-income kids, from one of dead-end jobs and minimum-wage employment to one where they will be able to succeed in the economic mainstream as professionals," explains Rafael Alvarez, founder of Genesys Works.

Alvarez was inspired to start the nonprofit in 2002 after spending years as a corporate strategist for a large corporation. On the side, he served on the board of a local charter school. That experience led him to an important conclusion: there are untapped opportunities in the corporate world for rudderless youth, if they're given a chance and pushed by high expectations.

Young people enter his program the summer prior to their senior year in high school. After eight weeks of intensive training they are given a year-long part-time job with one of many business partners. These are not make-believe slots, but paid positions with significant duties and chances to earn valuable experience.

"One thing the students learn very quickly is that Genesys Works is not a handout," Alverez says. "It's an opportunity. But they have to work at it."

All participants must be on track to graduate from high school and able to spend afternoons of their senior year on the job. The most important requirement is that they be eager to work. They are selected in cooperation with the Houston school system. The youngsters targeted are what Alvarez calls the "quiet middle"—not troublemakers or on the verge of dropping out, but also not excelling in life, so far. Many of these "middlers" will be the first in their families to graduate from high school.

The key mechanism that keeps the Genesys Works engine humming is an alliance with local businesses and corporations who provide the job placements. The nonprofit recognizes that their students must provide tangible benefits to the company at the same time that they are improving themselves.

"We help a company get a job done that they need anyway, at less cost than they would have to pay at a competing for-profit firm. And at the same time we have a social mission of changing the lives of students. So engaging clients is relatively easy," says Alvarez. Companies like Wells Fargo, ExxonMobil, GE Oil & Gas, and JPMorgan Chase work with the program, which saw 333 young people complete both its training and work portions in a recent school year.

Students are hired as independent contractors, not employees. The nonprofit bills the companies at a set rate, compensates its young people, and keeps a slice of revenue itself to fund its operating costs. The Houston chapter of Genesys Works gets about three quarters of its operating budget from contracting revenue. The remaining fourth comes from philanthropic investments by donors like the Houston Endowment, New Profit, and the Jenesis Group.

The Jenesis Group first supported Genesys Works in 2009 with operational capital and support for their building. They were attracted by its self-financing aspect, and appreciated that Genesys Works listens for the skills needed by the marketplace and responds accordingly, rather than just treating the internships like college-prep. The foundation helped launch a new Genesys Works chapter in San Francisco in 2012, and recently made a three-year, $3.5 million commitment to help Genesys Works strengthen its infrastructure so it can grow more aggressively in the future.

> Participants must sign an agreement that stipulates immediate expulsion for drug use, and a lower stipend for being even one minute late to class.

Already Genesys Works has expanded beyond Houston to the Twin Cities, Chicago, and, as mentioned, the Bay Area. The organization looks at four indicators before moving to a new city: a large population of students in need, a school system willing to form a partnership, businesses willing to hire, and a solid base of donors. In San Francisco, Genesys started with corporate support from AT&T and the Pacific Gas and Electric Company, and philanthropic seed money from the Greenlight Fund and Tipping Point.

There are other organizations that link at-risk kids to real-life work in ways similar to Genesys Works. Indeed, philanthropists anxious to support direct job placements as the surest route to helping struggling youngsters now have many models to choose from. Three additional examples are the Washington, D.C.-based Urban Alliance, Boston-born Year Up, and Taller San Jose in California.

Urban Alliance

Urban Alliance recruits its students from big-city high schools with some of the highest dropout rates in the United States. It exposes them to real work and gives them opportunities to succeed. It finds this can change lives.

The nonprofit has served more than 10,000 young people across its four locations. Its formula is built on the idea that the social isolation of young people who come from poor neighborhoods can have many detrimental effects. The group takes teenagers who often have never had a personal relationship with a model of success, and exposes them to the daily work done at corporations like Bank of America, Capital One, Morgan Stanley, Verizon, and Marriott.

Urban Alliance targets youngsters between their junior and senior years in high school. Low-income African-American and Latino students are the primary market. A minimum GPA of 2.5, being on track for graduation, and a positive attitude are required, excluding many students from the mix.

During the summer, those selected attend an unpaid, multi-week boot camp that teaches work skills. After successful training, they are placed in an entry-level part-time job at a major corporation. UA staff serve as career mentors, and contact students every week. Students remain in their jobs for nine months, typically working from 2 p.m. to 5 p.m. each weekday except for Fridays, when they attend ongoing professional workshops at Urban Alliance offices. These sessions include training in financial literacy, post-high-school planning, and life skills. Partway through the year, students get a job evaluation on 10 hard skills and 10 soft skills, reflecting the real-world realities of being in the paid work force. High-performing students are eligible for wage increases.

Many of these students are surrounded in the rest of their life by peers who encourage them to quit when challenges arise, says Nathaniel Cole, executive director of the Washington, D.C., chapter. The UA program pushes them to persevere through obstacles. "The great thing about our mentors is that we're challenging young people in areas where they haven't been challenged before," he states.

Students who complete the program are then connected to Urban Alliance's alumni-services staff, which stays in touch with them for the next four years. To date, Urban Alliance has shepherded 100 percent of its participants through high-school graduation, and 90 percent have gone on to attend college. Of those who start college, 80 percent remain enrolled at least through their second year.

Time management and financial literacy are two of the largest issues that Urban Alliance teaches. "The time management component is huge," notes Cole. "How to balance school, this job experience they've just signed on for, and then life." In addition, Urban Alliance throws more unusual items into the mix, such as healthy eating and exercising.

Urban Alliance relies on a revenue-generating component for much of its funding. For each student who participates in an internship, the hiring company makes a tax-deductible donation of $12,500 to Urban Alliance. The organization then pays the students $10 per hour. The residual retained by Urban Alliance doesn't cover the full cost of the program, but it dramatically reduces the additional philanthropic investment needed to keep the program operating.

One of Urban Alliance's greatest challenges is finding enough corporate partners. Often, the organization lacks enough job sites to offer every student who goes through pre-work the opportunity for an intern job. Students have to be put on a waiting list until a position opens.

Urban Alliance has branches in northern Virginia, Baltimore, and Chicago. When considering new chapters, the group considers community need, the availability of partners providing jobs, and practical factors like whether companies are accessible by public transportation. If the nonprofit can line up 70 paid jobs for students at the $12,500 level, they are willing to build a team and establish a presence in a new city.

Year Up

Shortly after he graduated from college in the late 1980s, Gerald Chertavian mentored, through the Big Brother program, a young man who lived in a public-housing project in Manhattan. The experience convinced him that too much human talent was being wasted among poor children. After the success of a company he co-founded, he used $500,000 of his own money and support from other donors to create a nonprofit aimed at linking young people from struggling families with productive workplaces.

The new organization Year Up was launched in Boston in 2000. It works with young people ages 18 to 24 with a high-school diploma or GED, but no clear next step in their lives. High-school guidance counselors and organizations like Big Brothers Big Sisters and the YMCA help identify candidates. It can be a tricky clientele: many of them Spanish-speaking, averaging 1.9 as a high-school GPA, and 780 as an SAT score. One crucial screen: participants must be "at-risk but not high-risk"—that is, not use drugs or have committed violent crime.

The program can be tough. It requires a detailed application, a writing sample, references, and two interviews. For every 100 young adults who say they are interested, only 25 will complete the application process, and only 10 will be accepted. Participants must sign an agreement that stipulates immediate expulsion for drug use, and a lower stipend for being even one minute late to class. Those accepted receive six months of full-time training. If they make it through that, they begin a six-month internship at a corporate partner, where most of them carry out computer-related jobs.

The training is described as "high-expectation, high-support." It addresses social and emotional development, time use, "behavior management," conflict resolution, personal finance, writing skills, and even current affairs, so graduates will be at home in a corporate environment. "To lower the bar is a disservice to our students," Chertavian adds. "It's disrespectful not to have high expectations."

> Making the program an attractive business proposition is the best way to recruit partnering firms.

Year Up participants receive staff advising on personal as well as professional issues, and are assigned a mentor from the business community. Students receive a $30-a-day stipend for living expenses while they are training (though they lose $25 of that if they are late for class). Once they begin working they get a weekly stipend of roughly $200, paid by the corporate partners—who also help Year Up itself defray roughly $2,000 out of the $11,000 annual cost per student. (The remaining expenses are covered by foundations, companies, and individual supporters.)

Year Up was designed partly to help corporations fill back-office jobs that they are having trouble finding adequate candidates for. Making the program an attractive business proposition is the best way to recruit partnering firms. More than 250 corporations across the country now collaborate with Year Up, which has become a reliable "pipeline" for some of the companies to graduate workers into technical, customer service, and sales positions.

"We often get pigeonholed as a charitable act, but we've built a $70 million business on providing corporate America with talent that they can hire," says Chertavian. The goal is for companies to hire their temporary placements after the Year Up training is complete. Even if they don't, the participant has a new toolbox of skills and a working track record that can be taken to the next career opportunity. He or she also earns between 18 and 30 college credit hours for completing the program.

Four months after graduation, 84 percent of Year Up participants are either working or attending college full time. The average wage of workers is $16 per hour. That's 30 percent more than a control group of peers outside the program earned.

By 2015, Year Up was training 2,700 students annually in 11 cities across the U.S. The key quality the program seeks in participants? Motivation. "We 'screen in' based on motivation," reports Chertavian. "If someone is motivated," he says, "in one year we can pretty much guarantee that they'll be in a livable-wage job."

Dealing with the toughest cases: Taller San Jose

Genesys Works, Urban Alliance, and Year Up target youth who are in the lower tier of achievement but have at least avoided active anti-social behavior. Taller San Jose focuses on an even more endangered cohort. It intervenes with troubled youths who are already involved with the criminal justice system, have a history of drug or alcohol abuse, or are otherwise on the road to conflict, failure, and dependence.

Taller San Jose (Spanish for "St. Joseph's Workshop"; Joseph being the patron saint of work) was founded in Orange County, California, in 1995 by a group of Catholic nuns. TSJ's mission is to train 18- to 28-year-old southern Californians who have gotten into trouble—many of them as gang members—in technical professions and life skills, with the ultimate goal of building life-long self-sufficiency. Every year, the group bears down on 350 of these difficult individuals, and since its launch it has helped 8,000 of them develop marketable skills and find employment. Fully 72 percent of enrollees are employed one year after graduating, at an average starting wage of $11.13 per hour.

TSJ's program has four main components:

- **Coaching**
  When young people first arrive, a specialist helps them establish a plan built around individual goals. One-on-one coaching and mentoring over a two-year period is a key component of the program.

- **Skill building**
  This technical training is focused on four industries—construction trades, health care, health-care administration, and business technology. Each young person is enrolled in a track that suits his or her interests and aptitudes.

- **Job placement and retention**
  TSJ has relationships with local employers looking for trained workers in one of the four industry tracks. After placement, continuing efforts help new hires keep their jobs and advance.

- **Career-to-education pathway**
  TSJ partners with community colleges and vocational schools to encourage continuing education that keeps workers current and helps them increase their wages and opportunities in the future.

For the first four to five months, skill-building is the main emphasis. The training is provided in an atmosphere like a workplace and treated as a job, with the trainees receiving a stipend. About 75 percent of those who start this portion of the program complete it. After that point, about 80 percent of the students persevere through the remaining employment and education components to complete the full program. Reflecting its challenging clientele, TSJ is a full two-year commitment—longer than others we have so far profiled.

Participants are not required to have a high-school diploma, and many don't. TSJ focuses more on basic skills—ability to read, write, and be responsible. Applicants accepted into TSJ must have math and literacy skills no higher than the fifth- to eighth-grade level. The rationale for this is that individuals with greater skills can rely on other resources like community colleges. TSJ is aimed at the most deficient populations, who will be left behind and forgotten without their intervention.

Of those who attend TSJ, 77 percent are unemployed, 65 percent are skills deficient, nearly all are low income. Many lack English-language skills, 27 percent have a criminal background, and 30 percent are parents.

The program works intensively with its charges all day every week day. Executive director Shawna Smith says the rigorous nature of the program makes it stand out from other job-training efforts. Building strong trusting relationships with the young people over a two-year period is crucial. When things start to go sideways, as they inevitably do, the young person knows that TSJ will support him, while also demanding good performance.

The other trademark of the program is treating businesses in the community as customers who need to be pleased. "We are very much informed by what local employers need in terms of skills," Smith says. "We are constantly looking at labor-market data to find growing industry sectors, what skill sets are needed there, and where there are skill gaps in our surrounding labor market."

The organization has always been funded primarily by private philanthropy. Some top donors include the Weingart Foundation and the California Wellness Foundation. "Private philanthropy has given us the freedom to respond to problems in the organization and fix them," Smith says. "If things aren't working, we're looking at why—what do we need to refine and adjust? Or do we need to get rid of that program? We can move pretty quickly. That's helped us build a successful model."

School-based paths to success: Pro-Vision

So far we've been looking at para-educational organizations, which swing into play to fill gaps and failures left behind by public schools. For donors interested in making investments within the education infrastructure, there are also worthwhile models to consider.

Building a whole school around workforce development is a tall order. It's also an exciting opportunity. What better way to reach at-risk young people on the virtues and satisfactions and life-importance of work than through school? Houston's Pro-Vision charter school is an intriguing example of how brick-and-mortar public education institutions can be dedicated to inculcating practical work skills.

Located in one of the more dangerous neighborhoods in the country, Pro-Vision is more than just a school—it's an oasis whose mission is to renew an entire urban community. After retiring from the NFL in 1988, former cornerback Roynell Young moved to Houston to start a business career. While driving the neighborhoods of south Houston with a potential client, Young saw many listless African-American young men who were involved in little more than gang life and the drug trade. Young decided to take action.

Young and co-founder Mike Anderson created Pro-Vision in 1990 as a youth mentorship organization and recruited an initial class of young men to be taught the importance of positive values, responsible manhood, and a strong work ethic. In 1995, Pro-Vision grew into a charter school. It started with 80 students in sixth through eighth grade, and touched the lives of 4,000 young men over the next two decades.

Today, Pro-Vision occupies a 21-acre campus. We had an opportunity to visit the school and see its operations first hand, and it is a dramatic outlier in what is otherwise the urban desert of south Houston. In addition to the school building, it has an urban garden, obstacle course, football field, basketball court, a nature-walk circling the perimeter of the property, and plenty of room for growth and expansion. For many of the African-American young men it trains, this might be their first exposure to homegrown vegetables, and high expectations.

> The first principle we practice here is that life owes you nothing. Everything is earned. If you do nothing, expect nothing.

The school was the first major investment in the surrounding Sunnyside neighborhood in many years. Young's view is that if he can help this part of Houston become healthy, "then the rest of Houston is super healthy." In addition to the charter school for middle- and high-school students, Pro-Vision operates a manhood academy designed to cultivate leadership, good character, and integrity among young males; an enterprise academy aimed at workplace success; and an urban farm intended to foster a strong work ethic.

Once students have completed the manhood-development classes, they are eligible to participate in the job-enterprise academy. In partnership with Houston corporations, the latter provides summer employment opportunities in a mix of blue-collar and white-collar positions. His young men rarely complain about their jobs, Young notes, because by that point they've had to work the urban garden in the sizzling heat of a Houston summer. To inculcate the importance of budgeting, Pro-Vision saves 25 percent of each student paycheck in an escrow account that can only be accessed in the future.

Young men work in part-time summer jobs Monday through Thursday each week. On Friday, they return to Pro-Vision for intensive workshops on financial literacy, business etiquette, and résumé writing. Like Genesys Works, Urban Alliance, and Year Up, this blend of real-world work and instructional time yields a mix of benefits—skills learned, contacts made, and improved rates of graduation from school. That package of results has high value.

Young lights up when he starts to talk Pro-Vision's successes. Nine out of ten boys who enter his middle school end up graduating from high school. And 97 percent of the young men who graduate from the charter high school, manhood program, and enterprise training go on to either attend college or trade school, get a job, or serve in the military.

Young describes the underlying approach of the program as demonstrating success to young men who have never experienced what success really tastes like. It's about teaching a new way of life—not just providing an education or job skills, but a new way of thinking and seeing the world. The teachers at Pro-Vision seek to eliminate any sense of entitlement from the students.

"Our kids are suffering from not understanding the process of success," Young says. "They see it on TV and on the Internet, but they don't understand the process. They don't know how to connect the dots. They don't know what the habits are. The first principle that we practice here is that life owes you nothing. The only thing that life gave you is that you're breathing, you're healthy, and you're of sound mind. Everything else is earned. Here, if you do nothing, expect nothing."

Using entrepreneurship to hook the young: BUILD, Juma, Dakota

An alternative to training young people to take jobs in big companies is to excite their entrepreneurial spirit. Surveys show that younger people have fewer inhibitions and more inclination to consider enterprising work. What would happen if those ambitions were tapped and encouraged among kids who are at economic risk?

Donors and foundations are finding out. In the late 1990s, legendary venture capitalist Franklin "Pitch" Johnson offered support to launch BUILD—a San Francisco Bay-area organization that uses the hook of entrepreneurship to entice at-risk young people into a life of fulfilling, self-supporting work. Today, BUILD enjoys strong support from the Coatue, New Profit, Tipping Point, and Michael & Susan Dell foundations, and the SalesForce.com, Wells Fargo, and PwC corporate foundations.

At sites in Boston and Washington, D.C. as well as northern California, BUILD provides a four-year high school program that can be taught in either charter schools or conventional public schools. It targets students who are likely to drop out of high school without an intervention.

BUILD gives these underperforming and disengaged students opportunities to conceive, design, and run businesses.

"The idea of creating a business and making money is appealing to these students," says Paul Collins, BUILD's Bay Area director.

In ninth grade, BUILD teaches youngsters how to work as a team on a business plan. They get four opportunities to present the plan to audiences at their school, then eventually take part in a business-plan competition at the end of their freshman year.

In tenth grade, the students begin to turn their business plan into a practical entity. They create executive roles and apportion responsibilities for manufacturing, sales, marketing, finance, and all other business-related details. They adapt their product according to feedback they get from the "marketplace" of other students.

A few of these business plans might lead to the launching of actual enterprises. And the process of creating them will get some students interested in particular work with existing firms. But actual commerce and short-term employment is not the goal. Excitement that leads the student to take ownership of his education and future direction is the goal.

While BUILD students are offered internships and career planning in their eleventh and twelfth grades, the first emphasis then is on preparing them for college. The program uses its entrepreneurial training as "experiential education" that motivates learning. It seems to work: Fully 96 percent of BUILD enrollees graduated from high school in 2014. And 84 percent of grads enrolled in four-year college, while another 11 percent continued their education in some other form. BUILD thus is principally a college-readiness program that uses entrepreneurship as a way to inspire young adults.

Another Bay Area charitable program takes a very different approach—involving at-risk youth directly in day-to-day business as a discipline, an opener of horizons, and a source of cold, hard cash. "The best social-service program in the world is a job," says Adriane Gamble Armstrong, the chief operating officer of Juma Ventures. "If we can connect a youth to work-force-development skills and an actual job with income, he or she has the ability to become a productive member of society."

The organization started in 1993 employing homeless teens at its own Ben & Jerry's franchise in San Francisco. Over the next few years it branched out to other scoop shops and then the sports-stadium concession business. In 1996 it earned a contract to sell food and drink at San Francisco's Candlestick Park, employing 40 young people.

"I'll never forget my second night out at Candlestick," writes one early student vendor. "It was about 30 degrees and raining. I was standing behind this cart, freezing. For the first half of the game I was standing there doing nothing. Then I looked up and I had this long line. My fingers curled up from holding the scoop, but I kept working. I was able to pace myself and get through the day, get my line down, get everything back to normal. I felt like I accomplished something that day."

The concession model took off, and since then, more than 4,000 kids have earned over $4 million at stadiums throughout the U.S. through Juma, gaining real work experience, money, and intensive life coaching from staff members, all at the same time.

Juma recruits students through partnerships with schools, social services agencies, and other nonprofits, choosing kids from that middle group who face obstacles but have the drive to take advantage of its programs. Those it accepts get help in three areas: employment, academic support, and financial literacy and asset building.

Participants hail from low-income families with no experience of higher education. Absent intervention, many would never graduate from high school, nevermind enroll in college. And among those from this demographic background who do make it to college, only a fifth typically complete a degree. By contrast, 97 percent of Juma students graduate from high school and 70 percent earn a college degree within five years.

Jonny Alejandre didn't want to go at first, but his mother urged him to attend the Juma Ventures presentation at his high school. "I don't know what would've happened if I hadn't agreed," says the 17-year-old junior. "It's so surreal that one small event can drastically change your life."

Before Juma, says Alejandre, "something 'umph' was missing" from his life. Now he's getting his "umph" by running up and down bleachers selling pizza and popcorn at AT&T Park in San Francisco, saving his paychecks for college. "The sporting venue is a hook for many young men, especially," says Armstrong. "Once they're in, we can involve them in our other programs." The students learn personal responsibility, cash handling, punctuality, prioritizing, dress, and communication.

"I learned so much at Juma Ventures—stuff I can use for the rest of my life," writes Loretta Gomes, another former Juma student. "If I would not have taken the class seriously I would have probably lost my job....When I graduated Juma I not only walked away with new skills and a better attitude, a brighter future. I walked away with pride in myself, a confidence of knowing that I could handle every task given to me at work."

Students put their paychecks in individual development accounts, with matching funds of up to three-to-one offered by Citibank, BlackRock, and other donors. The funds can be used for higher education and other approved expenses. Juma also provides tutoring, SAT prep, and application and financial aid guidance to get kids into college. And it offers continuing advice, services, and counseling once students are on campus.

George Roberts' REDF and the Charles and Helen Schwab Foundation have supported Juma from the start. Along with monetary gifts, supporters have pitched in with pro bono services to help Juma thrive and grow. Gap Inc. gives professional development workshops for the group's staff. The Surdna Foundation is helping Juma open new sites in Sacramento and Los Angeles. This assistance now allows Juma to serve 1,200 teens in cities stretching from San Diego to Seattle to New Orleans.

"Going through the program has really made me think about what I want to do, and how to use what I have in order to achieve those goals," says Alejandre. "It takes you out of your comfort zone and pushes you to be better, and grab the most potential out of yourself that you can."

A third effort to use the romance of small business ventures to touch kids not easily reached through traditional schooling is the work of the Dakota Foundation. In conjunction with the University of North Dakota Center for Innovation, the Dakota Foundation funds a series of two-week summer camps for Native American children. Their Entrepreneurship Education Program exposes middle- and elementary-school students to entrepreneurial thinking and career-building skills. The program is available on every Native American reservation in North Dakota and also in some public schools.

Bart Holaday, president of the Dakota Foundation, explains that this venture is an effort to help low-income Native American youth understand entrepreneurship. The Dakota Foundation will devote $600,000 to entrepreneurship education in 2015. "Our objective is to try to help people help themselves, through improving their skills and becoming more economically self sufficient," he says.

Mentorship as a pathway to success:
Colorado Uplift and Friends of the Children
A simple but often crunching obstacle faced by disconnected youth is their social environment. Detached from success, opportunity, and hope, often surrounded by non-work, drug abuse, risky sexual behavior, dependence, and a fatalistic view of life, many of them are trained in failure from an early age.

A single meaningful relationship with a successful person can sometimes make a difference. Research has shown the value of mentoring programs like Big Brothers Big Sisters. These reduce the likelihood that students will act in harmful ways or drop out of school. Mentorship is also used by some charitable programs to chip away at the problem of youth unemployment. Colorado Uplift and Friends of the Children are two examples.

Colorado UpLift was founded in 1982 to link troubled urban youths with jobs. But the founder soon discovered he was reaching young people too late in the process—many of them failed to show up or stick to their jobs once they got them. Earlier interventions were needed. Mentorship turned out to make a big difference. Today, Colorado UpLift is built on the premise that the core problem facing inner-city urban youths is a shortage of healthy relationships.

The best social-service program in the world is a job. The students learn personal responsibility, cash handling, punctuality, prioritizing, dress, and communication.

The organization pays full-time, credentialed staff to teach, coach, and guide young people. These staff develop long-term relationships as early as elementary school and continue them through middle school, high school, and early adulthood. Special emphasis is placed on character development, life skills, career preparation, and leadership. The aim is for each child to have at least one positive adult role model consistently throughout their teenage years.

"We never give up on students, despite what they might say or do," says Monique Jaramillo, a program manager for Colorado UpLift who herself came through the program in the early 1990s. "We love them through the bad and we love them through the good. We celebrate the good. We are those surrogate parents—father and mother figures—that are missing."

Programmatically, Colorado UpLift has four components.

- "In School" where 220 classes are held each week, right within the Denver public schools, teaching good character and life skills
- "After School" where staff use bonding activities and skill instruction to connect to kids

- "Adventure" where mentors and kids engage in outdoor activities
- And "Post-secondary" where the group preps students for college

The organization acknowledges that postsecondary education is not for everyone. They have a jobs-readiness program for high-school students looking to get a job right away that trains young people in how to interview, create a résumé, and act with poise and confidence.

Since its inception, Colorado UpLift has worked with 30,000 kids in the Denver area. Ninety percent of participants graduate from high school, and 86 percent go on to pursue either a four- or two-year college degree or vocational training. Every year, Colorado UpLift works with thousands of young people through the 260 classes it conducts in 27 Denver public schools. The intensive mentoring that links paid staff to kids on one-to-one bases is available to a smaller subset of kids as it is obviously expensive. Under the nonprofit Elevate USA, the program has been introduced to four other states: Florida, Arizona, New York, and Oregon.

To retain operating independence, the organization does not accept government grants. It relies on foundation support. Most recently, the Anschutz, Lewis Family, and Peieris foundations and the Daniels Fund have been substantial supporters of the Denver organization.

Another successful mentoring organization was founded by donor Duncan Campbell. For him, the issue of children growing up under stress is a personal one. His childhood family had two alcoholic parents; his dad went to prison twice; they subsisted on welfare. "I didn't want any other child to have the life that I had," Campbell says.

Despite his troubled background, Campbell succeeded in business. He founded a timber investment firm, sold the company in the early 1990s, then turned his thoughts to philanthropy. He hired a child psychologist to help him research the best ways to reach and help children from troubled backgrounds. Their conclusion: An early exposure to a positive adult role model was crucial. That's when Friends of the Children was born in Portland, Oregon, starting in 1993 with three social workers and 24 participating youngsters.

The FOTC model pairs threatened children with trained, paid full-time mentors—called "friends"—from kindergarten through twelfth grade. The friends aim to make sure that their charges progress through school, aren't incarcerated, and don't get pregnant out of wedlock. Mentors take on no more than eight children each, so that they are able to give each their full attention for no less than four hours each week.

Obviously that is an expensive proposition. Cognizant of costs, FOTC seeks out the youngsters who are most endangered. Their "reverse draft" allows the organization to serve young people with real troubles, who are highly likely to end up in trouble absent some intervention. Friends of the Children has mentored almost 1,000 of such children since its beginning.

"The entire program is built on the relationship that the friend develops with the child," Campbell says. "They learn a work ethic. Every child does some sort of work at every age level, such as selling lemonade or cutting a lawn or serving coffee." Working side-by-side with their charges, mentors assist with homework, teach skills like cooking and doing laundry, and inculcate social graces and constructive attitudes.

FOTC has expanded beyond Oregon. The organization currently serves over 800 children in five cities: Portland, New York, Boston, Seattle, and Klamath Falls, Oregon. A Microsoft employee helped bring the organization to Seattle. Lawyers and judges introduced it to New York City. A venture capitalist brought the program to Boston. Thanks to an offshoot of the Eckerd Family Foundation, an affiliated group using the core of the FOTC curriculum is now operating in Tampa Bay, Florida.

Duncan Campbell's family foundation launched Friends with three investments totaling around $2 million. Campbell gradually pared down his investments as larger foundations jumped on board and individual donors and businesses began to underwrite the group. Recent supporters include the Hearst, Robert Wood Johnson, Thrive, and Edna McConnell Clark foundations, the May & Stanley Smith Charitable Trust, and the M. J. Murdock Charitable Trust.

The biggest obstacle facing FOTC is the very high costs of its intensive paid mentoring—nearly $10,000 per child annually. Campbell acknowledges this is a brake on the program, but notes there are savings to society when the program is effective. "Friends of the Children breaks the cycle of poverty," he argues. "It breaks the cycle of kids dropping out. It breaks the cycle of kids being in the juvenile justice system, and the cycle of teen parenting."

Participating children graduate from high school at an 83 percent rate, even though 60 percent of their parents lack a high-school degree. While 50 percent have a parent who has been incarcerated, 93 percent of participating kids stay clear of the juvenile justice system. And although 85 percent of them were born to a teenage parent, 98 percent of mentees avoid early childbirth.

Working Around Homelessness, Substance Abuse, Disability

Donors trying to create pathways to work for "the least of these" can't ignore the homeless, addicted, or disabled. These populations face some of the very highest obstacles to self-reliance. How can a would-be worker obtain and maintain a job without consistent housing? Work is likewise hard to impossible for someone enslaved by drugs or alcohol. People with significant mental or physical disabilities may find it hard to get started, or to advance, at a job. Sometimes these afflictions overlap. A large proportion of the homeless face substance addictions, and many experience mental illness. Similarly, substance abuse can lead to disability. These are difficult populations that philanthropists must have strategies to address.

Gospel Rescue Missions

According to the National Alliance to End Homelessness, nearly 600,000 people experience homelessness on any given night in the U.S. Family meltdown, mental illness, or substance abuse is usually behind this end-state. The homeless person's primary concern usually is finding food and a place to spend the night. Employment falls further down the list. Not surprisingly, most homeless persons are unemployed.

Donors have been involved in combating homelessness through America's network of local gospel rescue missions since the late-1800s. There are 300 of these quietly effective facilities across the country. They provide a warm and safe place to sleep for the night, a hot meal, rehabilitation services for about 18,000 alcoholics and addicts every year, and faith-based instruction. Some also work to create clear pathways to employment.

For example, the Raleigh Rescue Mission, located in North Carolina's capital city, provides not only emergency services but also longer-term training and vocational opportunities to help the homeless establish a sustainable style of living. In New York City, the Bowery Mission offers the basics of food, shelter, and clothing for men and women coming off the streets, but doesn't stop there. It also has a residential recovery program that provides services to beat addiction, personal counseling and mentorship, and education and employment training.

The Union Gospel Mission in Spokane, Washington, offers vocational training as part of its recovery curriculum. UGM assesses each participant's skills and strengths, then puts him on a career path matching his vocational bent. Participants work 240 hours in unpaid positions at collaborating businesses, then use this experience to procure paid employment.

Rescue Ministries of Mid-Michigan, Wheeler Mission Ministries in Indianapolis, and Denver Rescue Mission are three more missions that offer vocational training. More gospel missions are moving beyond the traditional rescue function, and beyond even job-placement efforts, and pushing into active programming that prepares individuals with highly problematic employment histories for occupational success.

"If we don't take the next step of helping mission guests be assimilated back into society, then we haven't fully succeeded," says John Ashmen, president of the Association of Gospel Rescue Missions, the largest and oldest network of faith-based shelters in the U.S.

Most cities have a local rescue mission that does wonderful, unsung work aiding some of our country's most miserable people. One way that donors could have a quick impact is to provide funding that allows their local mission to offer some of the workforce-development components developed in places like New York, Spokane, Indianapolis, and Denver. Tapping into an existing, proven apparatus like America's rescue mission network can be an efficient way to reap significant social dividends.

Social enterprising: Delancey Street, FareStart

Three blocks north of AT&T Park, home to the 2014 world champion San Francisco Giants, sits a 360,000 square foot compound right on the Embarcadero waterfront. Sporting a beautiful view of the bay, the Delancey Street Foundation hums with activity. On the street side, visitors find a nicely appointed restaurant, complete with breakfast, lunch, and dinner menus. White-collar workers from nearby businesses sit enjoying delicious fare. Occasionally, the ding of a trolley car can be heard as it rolls by just outside the windows.

But something is different about this restaurant. All of the employees have troubled backgrounds, including homelessness, gang activity, substance abuse, and incarceration. Yet here they are, working side by side to make the restaurant a success. And the restaurant is only one of many microenterprises housed within DSF. Sometimes known as "Harvard for the underclass," the Delancey Street Foundation works to elevate strugglers into the middle class by preparing them for the world of middle-class work, including encouraging traditional middle-class values.

Founded in 1971, DSF has graduated more than 18,000 participants. According to Mimi Silbert, DSF's longtime president, the main goal is to transform residents from a self-focused attitude to a selfless one. That's partly accomplished through the DSF model: the nonprofit relies almost exclusively on residents—those former gang members and drug addicts— to make the organization run, not paid staff. If that concept sounds crazy to you, you're not alone. But the results have been impressive.

Rather than relying primarily on philanthropy or government for operating funds, DSF generates approximately 70 percent of its operating budget from its own social enterprises—the businesses operated on-site exclusively by residents. In addition to the Delancey Street Restaurant, DSF has a coffee house called Crossroads Café that could be easily mistaken for a Starbucks or Panera Bread. (In fact, Pottery Barn CEO Howard Lester donated the furniture and dishes inside.) And in one corner there is a bookstore and a gallery with works of art created by residents.

Located in the very center of the DSF grounds is a 146-seat movie theater that is often rented by private parties for events. In addition, movie producers use the screening room to review their day's work for films shot in San Francisco. The theater lobby has a glass-enclosed bar often rented (with serving staff) for events.

> All of the employees have troubled backgrounds, yet here they are, working side by side to make the restaurant a success.

In addition to these glitzy elements, DSF offers a plethora of practical services under its social-enterprise umbrella: moving services; automotive repair and detailing; catering; event and wedding planning; Christmas tree sales; commercial decorating; digital printing, banners, silk screen, and framing; upholstering and sewing; woodworking and furniture making; construction and property management; corporate transportation services including limos; and warehousing.

DSF's only major requirements for those who desire to enter the program are that they possess a strong motivation to change and be in reasonably good health. People who have already got their act together are sent elsewhere. "We have to feel that no one else will take them," says Silbert. DSF does ban sex offenders and those who require psychiatric medication.

Applicants can stop by the DSF location any time, day or night, but they are required to sit on a bench in a waiting room until the interview begins. It is intended to be a first screen for cooperation and self-discipline. Sometimes arrivals must wait for hours. Nearly nine out of 10 applicants to DSF come through the criminal justice system. Former prisoners are required to write a letter of introduction before they are evaluated for an interview.

"We do not talk about people's problems," Silbert says. "We believe in finding their strengths. Change is a verb. If you want to change, do.

Don't sit there and talk about how hard it was growing up. We know it was terrible, but there are people born without arms and legs and they figure out a way to live. So you're going to have to figure out a way to live, and we're going to teach it to you."

Once admitted, a resident commits to stay for at least two years. The average tenure is four years. The three "house rules" are no drugs or alcohol, no violence, and no threats. While at DSF, residents can receive the equivalent of a GED, along with specific training in marketable skills acquired through the social enterprises outlined above. Residents are also taught social skills. When residents are prepared to graduate from the program into the "real work world," they find a job off-site but continue to live on the DSF campus and pay rent until achieving full stability.

For training and instruction, DSF relies on an "each one, teach one" model. As soon as a resident can read at an eighth-grade level, he teaches someone who is reading at a sixth-grade level—and then on down the line. If a resident works in the kitchen as a prep cook, then he's training and mentoring a dishwasher. This approach ensures that while residents are acquiring technical capabilities they are also learning social cooperation and leadership.

In addition to its San Francisco anchor facility, DSF has five other locations: in Los Angeles; the San Juan Pueblo Indian reservation of New Mexico; Greensboro, North Carolina; Brewster, New York; and Stockbridge, Massachusetts.

Numerous examples of impressive social-enterprise-centered non-profits now exist. In addition to DSF and others already mentioned, we will discuss many more in subsequent pages. Another worth mentioning here because of its similarity to the Delancey Street Foundation is FareStart, located in Seattle. It operates a restaurant that employs homeless men and women. It is built around a 16-week training program in which students learn the culinary arts alongside experienced chefs, while producing as many as 2,500 meals each day. FareStart also has a barista training program specifically geared toward homeless young adults in Seattle. Along with its on-the-job training FareStart provides instruction in life skills, personalized guidance, and job placement services.

Social enterprise in NYC: the Doe Fund

By sheer numbers, New York City has the largest population of homeless individuals in the U.S.—over 64,000 in 2013, according to the U.S. Department of Housing and Urban Development. Los Angeles is a close second at nearly 53,000 individuals. A big difference between the two, of course, is weather: The homeless in New York City must deal with freezing temperatures for months at a time.

It was winter bitterness that gave birth to the Doe Fund. In the early 1980s when New York City was at an economic and social nadir, winter cold killed several homeless persons. In response, donors launched the Doe Fund, named for one of the women who froze to death, known only as "Mama Doe." A single principle served as its lodestar: the homeless have "the potential to be contributing members of society."

Work is what translates this into reality. Doe trains people to be useful, do for themselves, and achieve self-sufficiency. In most homeless shelters and addiction recovery centers, notes Doe staffer Alexander Horwitz, the goal is just to sustain life. "That's not our objective. Our objective is to give these folks back their lives so that they can live independently and self-sufficiently."

If a homeless individual wants to join the program, the first requirement is that he give up any sense of entitlement. At the Doe Fund, everything must be earned. To encourage a new identity, all individuals are referred to as "trainees" after they are admitted, rather than "homeless."

The average length of stay for participants is nine months. The first requirement is that residents work at the shelter they occupy. Some prepare meals, learning cooking skills in the process. Soon they are enmeshed in the Doe Fund's paid work program—called Ready, Willing & Able—which provides transitional jobs at wages between $8.20 and $8.95 per hour in areas like building maintenance, pest control, commercial driving, back office work. One of the Doe Fund's biggest revenue-generating social enterprises is street cleaning in New York City. Doe's "men in blue" clean 170 miles of streets each day, 365 days a year. "These are people who go from sleeping on the streets to cleaning them," smiles Horwitz.

The daily structure and sense of accomplishment that work provides has powerful effects in bringing order to the lives of many Doe participants. This prepares them for outside employment and mainstream life in a way that free welfare services are unable to do. In addition, the in-house businesses give the nonprofit a steady revenue stream to help pay for its services.

Strugglers graduate from Ready, Willing & Able once they are drug free, have a private-sector job, an apartment, and are paying child support if needed. For job placements, the Doe Fund allies with nearly 400 private-sector small businesses, hospitals, and companies. "It was always our intention to avoid establishing a workforce of people who could not get a job anywhere else," co-founder and former businessman George McDonald told us. "We've always focused on transitioning into the larger American economy. We didn't have to create any economic system for them to go into: We have the best one in the world."

Seventy percent of Doe's program staff are themselves graduates of its program. "These individuals have gotten married and had children and earn a very good living. They are the proof to other participants that change is possible," says McDonald's wife and co-founder, Harriet Karr-McDonald.

In addition to being homeless, Doe's participants are overwhelmingly minorities, 70 percent have a criminal record, and 85 percent have been substance abusers. Yet more than 60 percent of the persons who enter Ready, Willing & Able graduate into independent life and employment. A 2010 Harvard study found ex-cons coming out of the program were 60 percent less likely to have another felony conviction within three years after leaving prison.

A third of the Doe Fund's $52 million annual budget comes from revenue generated by the social enterprises. Another third comes from government—a percentage that Karr-McDonald is always working to reduce. The final third originates from private philanthropy. With funds from grantors like the Robin Hood, Hecksher, Andrew Mellon, Edna McConnell Clark, May and Samuel Rudin, Starr, and Achelis & Bodman foundations, among other institutional grantors, along with around 55,000 individuals who have given money to the fund at some point in its history, Doe has grown and expanded into multiple locations, programs, and businesses.

One graduate, a multiple felon now pursuing a college degree, says his experience with the Doe Fund "was the first time that I was told what I could do for myself." Could this guiding principle make Doe a model for future poverty alleviation? Co-founder Harriet Karr-McDonald says yes. "Work works. We believe that we can change the welfare paradigm in America through work and opportunity."

More social enterprising: Homeboy Industries

Another pioneering group successfully offering job training to tough populations through its own social enterprises is Homeboy Industries. Headquartered in downtown Los Angeles, Homeboy houses numerous social enterprises, including Homeboy Bakery, Homegirl Café, a catering business, a T-shirt silkscreen and embroidery operation, a gourmet food truck, a diner, farmers'-market stands, and online stores. These businesses offer perches where persons needing job training can get experience. And their cash flow also helps subsidize the many services Homeboy offers to the difficult clients who come through its doors: substance-abuse support, legal help, mental health treatment, domestic violence cessation, a charter high school, even a very successful solar-panel installment training program.

The seeds for Homeboy Industries were planted two decades ago by a Jesuit priest, Father Greg Boyle. Assigned to Dolores Mission—a heavily Latino parish in one of the poorest and most violent communities in L.A.—Boyle grew tired of losing young people to senseless gang violence. He began to seek out gang members and offer spiritual direction, retreats, and personal prayers. Boyle also realized early on that getting kids out of gangs and helping them become productive members of society would require jobs. In 1988, while still pastor of Dolores Mission, he created "Jobs for a Future," which grew into Homeboy Industries.

The program is particularly devoted to getting gang-bangers off the streets, training and rehabilitating them to the point where they can

> We've always focused on transitioning into the larger American economy. We didn't have to create any economic system for them to go into: We have the best one in the world.

get, and keep, meaningful employment. About a thousand former gang members and recently incarcerated persons come to Homeboy every month seeking services and job help. At any given time, up to 300 former gang associates are employed in one of Homeboy's programs. Fully 85 percent of Homeboy clients are on parole or probation.

Homeboy works closely with Los Angeles businesses to channel people who come for help into private-sector jobs. Clients with bad records, weak skills, or poor work habits often start at one of the Homeboy's own enterprises. There, participants learn how to show up on time, treat a customer with courtesy, and exhibit professionalism. Once they have established a good record and useful skill set there, the program helps place them in a market job.

While sales by the social enterprises generate close to $5 million dollars of annual revenue to help underwrite programming, Homeboy still relies on more than $8 million dollars of annual fundraising. Dozens of foundations and major individual donors provide support. More than a hundred foundations and individual donors made important long-term contributions to the growth of Homeboy Industries during their first 25 years, including the Annenberg, Robert Wood Johnson, Ahmanson, Weingart, Hilton, Keck, Irvine, Walmart, and Parsons foundations.

Work-friendly solutions to substance abuse: Step 13 and Teen Challenge

Alcohol is our most abused drug—one fourth of U.S. adults report engaging in binge drinking during the past month, and an estimated 18 million Americans suffer from alcohol dependence. But 52 million Americans have also used prescription drugs for nonmedical reasons (6 million of them within the last month), and there are about 20 million annual users of marijuana today. In 2013, an estimated 2 million Americans used cocaine in 2013, 700,000 used heroin, and more than 500,000 took methamphetamine. These behaviors interfere with work in many ways.

For one thing, many employers now conduct drug testing on employees, especially in the lower-tier occupations that economic strugglers typically enter. Another barrier to work for drug users and alcohol abusers is simply the performance-damaging aspects of impairment. And then there is the fact that substance abusers often get snarled up in chaos, family breakup, and crime.

Work, however, can be an aid to walking away from all this. A satisfying job can push aside reliance on these compounds. That can be seen in two drug-rehab nonprofits that use reintegration into work as a strong part of their services.

Today, downtown Denver's Larimer Street is an eclectic assortment of restaurants, bars, and shops. That's a testament to the power of neighborhood revitalization, because three decades ago Larimer Street was a hub for drug dealers, prostitutes, and the homeless. The street was known as Denver's skid row.

It was in that turbulent atmosphere that Step 13 was born. A play off the traditional twelve steps of addiction recovery, Step 13 offers more than a typical recovery program. It requires work, and offers opportunities to succeed at it.

Step 13 was founded in 1983 by Bob Cote to help hard-core drunks and addicts transition away from life on the street, partly through the power of honest labor. A physically imposing, larger-than-life former boxer who passed away in 2013, Cote was himself a recovered alcoholic. He knew first-hand the torments of the men he was serving. And philanthropists impressed with his leadership—like Phil Anschutz, Steve Schuck, and the Daniels Fund—became generous supporters of his program.

As a residential program, Step 13 caters to males over the age of 21 who have lost everything due to their drug or alcohol addictions. Persons convicted of violent or sexual offenses are not admitted. Over the past three decades, more than 2,500 men have participated in the program, with an average enrollment time of nine months. They are taught to respect others, to work, and to sustain themselves.

The program provides training and job placement services, along with classes on such issues as budgeting, healthy relationships, cooking, and personal fitness. Residents are required to be out working or seeking employment during all weekdays. For those who can't find steady jobs, Step 13 hires them out as day laborers until they can land something more permanent. This program is known as StepWork.

Step 13 also offers in-house opportunities to acquire work skills, including their own social enterprises. One of the organization's best-known programs is DetailWorks—a car, truck, RV, and motorcycle detailing program staffed by shelter residents. Customers can either drop their vehicle off at Step 13's Larimer Street facility, or have Step 13 detailers come to them. A popular option created by the nonprofit allows baseball fans to leave their car at Step 13 for detailing while they catch a Rockies game at nearby Coors Field. In addition to getting back a slicked-up vehicle, they avoid the expensive stadium parking fees. Step 13 also accepts donated cars and trucks for rehab and resale.

As a residential program, Step 13 has a zero-tolerance policy for alcohol or substance use among enrolled men. This is enforced with daily testing. In addition, residents must support themselves either through an outside job, StepWork, or one of the social enterprises. Each man must pull his own weight.

There are no program costs for participants, but men must pay $10 a day (or $60 per week prepaid) to reside on the premises, and they buy their own food and cook in the communal kitchen. Men are also asked to handle routine maintenance at the facility. Monday through Thursday evenings, each man attends a mandatory meeting based on Alcoholics Anonymous.

In a partnership with Wells Fargo Bank, every participant opens a bank account. For some, this is the first one they've had. The organization conducts budgeting classes and teaches residents how to handle their earnings. This too helps connect the men to the world of success and self-sufficiency.

Step 13 serves about 80 men on any given day. "A lot of times, the identity of our men has come to be based not on who they are, but on what they've done in the past," says director Peter Droege (formerly of the Daniels Fund), who is the program's only paid staff member. "That's where we begin. Reminding them that success is about who they are today."

Many of these men's worldviews are also warped by entitlement payments, which can likewise come to define their lives, according to Droege. "Once they get onto an entitlement program, that's often their highest priority. They stand in lines, or limit their work hours, or adjust their behavior in order to maintain their entitlement. In that sense, entitlement is very similar to addiction."

The temptation of lifetime payments has convinced many Americans with disabilities to retreat into dependence on government checks when they could be supporting themselves and earning crucial social and psychological benefits of work as well.

Another drug rehabilitation program that uses workforce-readiness as an important part of recovery is Teen Challenge USA. It's a national program that offers teens, and also adults, residential rehabilitation. Founded in 1958 by Pastor David Wilkerson, Teen Challenge is one of the oldest faith-based addiction recovery programs in the country. Wilkerson's work in New York City convinced him that teens needed to make long-term commitments to wean themselves off drugs and alcohol. So he developed a residential program that would offer young people a combination of a strong sense of community, faith supports built on Bible study, and practical training in job skills that could support and stimulate the person occupationally.

Today, Teen Challenge is a network of over 1,100 centers worldwide. We had the opportunity to visit the Teen Challenge chapter headquartered in Denver, Colorado. The men's program, 180 Ministries, is housed in a two-story building in south Denver where residents spend 12 to 18 months learning new skills and turning their lives around. Eighty percent of its referrals come through churches. The most commonly abused drugs here are prescription medicines.

As part of the 180 Ministries program, young men participate in a "work therapy" initiative, which places them in jobs across a network of businesses in the Denver area. Similar ventures offer addiction-recovery services and work to young women (the House of Promise) and to single mothers (New Hope House). Teen Challenge charges individuals around $2,000 for treatment, but subsidizes those who can't meet the full bill. Local chapters rely on donations—from churches, individuals, businesses, and corporate partners. Foundation grants make up a final 10 percent of funding.

Helping disabled veterans find work

As we explored briefly in Chapter 2, the U.S. has experienced soaring disability claims in recent years. In the face of many medical and pharmacological miracles that reduce disabling conditions, in the face of sharply reduced injury thanks to improved workplace safety, in the face of myriad legal, technological, and attitudinal changes that have made it easier for persons who are disabled to be active in mainstream society, we are nonetheless faced with a disability explosion today. Hard-won achievements have been tragically counterbalanced by the destructive economic incentives of disability transfers. The temptation of lifetime payments has convinced many Americans to retreat into dependence on government checks when they could be actively supporting themselves and earning the crucial social and psychological benefits of work as well.

This is expensive for taxpayers. But it is disastrous for the long-term well-being of the disabled. The unintended effect of just giving people money rather than helping them earn their own independence is to diminish many people—defining them by their weaknesses rather than by their capacities and potential.

One of the saddest places where this trend is evident is among veterans. Young men and women with above-average inherent capabilities (which, statistically, veterans are) and deep maturing experience (which many vets accumulate) should be valuable additions to the American workforce and society when they leave military service. But perverse disability incentives are now ensnaring many veterans and getting in the way of their healthy reintegration. Nearly half of all post-9/11 veterans are now on track to claim disability payments when they leave the service, and they are claiming an average of nearly four maladies each. Among World War II troops, only one out of nine filed for disability, claiming less than two conditions on average. Those who deployed and those who stayed home, office-bound clerks and combat troops, men who faced bullets and men who repaired trucks—all types of vets are being swept up in this explosion of disability entitlements.

Daniel Gade, a West Point graduate who was awarded two Purple Hearts and lost a leg in Iraq, has noted that a disabled veteran in his early 20s can be eligible for $3,000 to $4,000 per month in disability payments, much of it tax free and much of it taken away if he finds work. Many of the entry-level jobs available to young people can't compare with that payment. And it can be received without labor, without any expectation or requirement for getting treatment that will improve one's condition and allow independence. This is an entitlement that will be paid for an entire lifetime.

As this book is written, The Philanthropy Roundtable is incubating a major experiment that seeks to create a healthier set of incentives for injured veterans. Among a group of several hundred veteran volunteers, it proposes to use donor support to turn our current disability compensation system on its head and then test the results. Instead of trickling out a lifetime of marginal monthly benefits, this experiment would front-load the process—spending generously on injured veterans as they leave the service to help them qualify themselves for their dream job and then expecting them to be contributing members of society instead of passive benefit collectors the rest of their lives.

With initial design support from the Anschutz, Milbank, Daniels, and Wilf foundations, this proposal will carefully track outcomes for vets. The front-loaded, work- and independence-based assistance will be compared to outcomes among vets drawing conventional disability benefits. Findings from the $10 million donor-funded experiment could then be used to make the federal system for disabled veterans friendlier to work and self-reliance.

In the meantime, there are hundreds of small philanthropic programs that aim to help veterans transition in healthy ways into the civilian workforce. One successful example is the Entrepreneurial Bootcamp for Veterans with Disabilities, operated with extensive donor support by Syracuse University. Mike Haynie, a U.S. Air Force veteran and professor of entrepreneurship at Syracuse's Whitman School of Management, founded the program in 2006.

EBV begins with a monthlong online course that teaches the basics of starting one's own business. This is followed by nine days of intensive classroom instruction. The participating veterans develop their own business plans and make presentations to a panel of business experts. Every aspect of creating, launching, and operating an entrepreneurial endeavor is covered. Graduates of the program then have access to a year's worth of free technical assistance from EBV trainers as they translate their effort into a real business.

It costs $5,280 to put each veteran through this course. Participants attend tuition-free though, thanks to generous support from individual donors, corporations, and foundations. To date, 600 veterans have completed the program, spawning many successful ventures and careers, even from vets with the most serious injuries. The boot camp has now been expanded to eight partner universities across the country, with Syracuse University keeping a tight rein on the quality of the programming by training instructors and sharing curriculum.

Donors interested in a venture-philanthropy approach also have another top-notch model to draw inspiration from. The Call of Duty Endowment (CODE) largely is funded by Activision Blizzard, the video-game company responsible for the best-selling Call of Duty series. CODE funds over a dozen top-rated nonprofits scattered across the country to link returning veterans with employment opportunities. Its goal is to put 25,000 veterans into high-quality jobs before the end of 2017.

Robert Kotick, president of Activision Blizzard, wants his firm's charitable efforts for veterans to reflect the realities of work in the business economy and to center on ways of helping post-9/11 veterans find lasting, productive jobs. Nonprofits apply to CODE through an application that requires details on things like what it costs for them to place a veteran and the average quality of their placements (defined by starting salary, full-time vs. part-time, industry, job functions, and so forth).

After CODE culls the applications, staff pass the best ideas to an outside board of advisers who whittle the list down to finalists. The auditing-consulting firm Deloitte then goes on site for two to five days to verify the nonprofit's claims, interview leadership teams, investigate the organization's financial health, and check on operations. The average resulting grant is approximately $400,000. CODE views the grant recipient as a business partner, and expects results from them on behalf of veterans.

Since CODE's founding in 2009, the organization has made $4.1 million in grants to 22 different organizations. From the program's beginning, it has helped place thousands of veterans in jobs, at an accelerating pace in recent months. CODE supported 5,600 placements in 2014 alone. The average starting salary for these placements was $45,000. In the early years, the cost-per-placement was around $1,500; now it is under $1,000.

"We feel that our process allows us to identify winners—nonprofits that are making an outsized impact," says CODE executive director Dan Goldenberg. This includes work with veterans with the most severe disabilities. In April 2014, for instance, CODE gave a $250,000 expansion grant to the Veterans Staffing Network run by Easter Seals to assist wounded warriors emerging from Walter Reed Hospital and Fort Belvoir Community Hospital.

Goodwill Industries helps place more than a quarter of a million hard-to-employ people in private jobs every year. It estimates that the workers it assists in any given year increase their lifetime earning potential by $15 billion.

Another nonprofit supported by CODE is the U.S. Veterans Initiative (U.S. VETS) headed by Vietnam veteran Stephen Peck. Ninety-two percent of the veterans placed in jobs by U.S. VETS are homeless, and many of them face physical and mental barriers. U.S. VETS tackles their issues in ways similar to how other top workforce-development organizations work: a mix of classroom instruction, interview training, case management, job fairs, and placement assistance. CODE made its initial $500,000 gift to U.S. VETS in 2013.

Goldenberg thinks the most pressing need for the future is showing private companies why it is in their interests to hire vets. "All the talk of patriotic duty and how great veterans are, it's wonderful and it makes you feel good. But what's important at the end of the day is seeing that these people are embraced as valuable assets in our civilian economy, so they and their employers can flourish together," he says.

For more information on workforce opportunities for returning veterans, we recommend *Serving Those Who Served: A Wise Giver's Guide to*

Assisting Veterans and Military Families, a manual published by The Philanthropy Roundtable and written by its full-time program manager for veteran affairs, Thomas Meyer.

Putting persons with serious mental or physical disabilities to work: Goodwill

An estimated 80 percent of individuals with severe mental or physical disabilities are not currently in the labor force. The obstacles to work faced by this cohort are perhaps the most difficult of any explored in this guidebook. Persons with serious afflictions, and combinations of physical and mental special needs, particularly need opportunities and assistance.

The good news is that philanthropists are making inroads in this area. (So too are some private companies that have established programs to hire and retain special-needs workers. Walgreens, for example, recently launched a nationwide push to train disabled persons for employment in its national chain of drug stores.)

The most common special-needs disabilities include autism, Down syndrome, mental retardation, cerebral palsy, and attention deficit/hyperactivity disorder. Sheltered workshops are one oft-used pathway to work for special-needs individuals. There are also efforts to integrate disabled workers into the regular workforce.

No group has done more to pioneer pathways to employment for special-needs men and women than Goodwill Industries. Goodwill operates as a network of independent local operations, organized and assisted by a national member-services center. In 2015 there were 165 of these independently run affiliates throughout the U.S. and Canada. They collect donated clothing, shoes, books, DVDs, furniture, and other household items, which they then organize, clean, rehabilitate, and sell through more than 3,000 retail outlets (plus an online auction site). Retail sales bring in close to $4 billion for the organization.

In addition, Goodwill organizes workers—those with special needs, along with persons with criminal backgrounds, and other hard-to-employ individuals—into teams that provide industrial and service work on a contract basis. Goodwill outlets carry out maintenance, landscaping, recycling, document management, and other tasks on an outsourced basis. This work brings in about $650 million of annual revenue.

Goodwill pours 83 percent of its earned revenues directly into programming. In addition to training and overseeing workers at its own stores and workshops, Goodwill helps place more than a quarter of a million hard-to-employ people in private jobs every year. It offers special-needs individuals personalized job coaching, help completing high school, and other aid. Some affiliates even operate charter high schools, or assist in the earning of vocational credentials in areas like fire-fighting and nursing. Social and financial resources are also offered, like help locating housing, financial literacy classes, and guidance on avoiding domestic abuse. Goodwill estimates that the workers it assists and trains in any given year increase their lifetime earning potential by $15 billion.

"We really look at our whole workforce as transitional," says Midwestern Goodwill executive Kent Kramer. "They might be transitioning into a higher paying job within Goodwill, or outside Goodwill. Our overarching mission is to move people toward economic self-sufficiency and break the cycle of poverty for that individual, for that family. We do that through education. We're proud that we offer employment opportunities to people no one else will."

Coping with mental illness at Fountain House

Only about 15 percent of people with serious mental illness are currently employed. This is an area dominated by government services and mandates, but private initiatives can make a difference here. Fountain House in New York City is an example. Created in 1948 by a group of patients recently released from a state hospital, the organization is built around giving the mentally ill the opportunity to work and live independently.

In addition to providing a "blanket" of community, education, fitness, and housing resources (500 people get temporary supported housing), Fountain House has a job-readiness component that has been a top priority since its founding. Through partnerships with various area businesses, it provides two job tracks. Transitional Employment offers temporary jobs of up to six months that allow members to build up their résumé. Supported Employment provides full-time or part-time positions that are ongoing. One ingredient in Fountain House's recipe of success is that if one of their placements doesn't show up for work, the organization will supply a replacement employee to fill the gap. That increases the willingness of employers to give the group's members an opportunity.

Fountain House also encourages entrepreneurial thinking and small-business creation in its training. It has a microbusiness incubator, called Linking Lives Enterprises, that has created four social ventures: Jack Rabbit Deliveries, Bluebird Designs, Clever Cheetah Catering, and

Rock Dove Industrial Services. Each of these businesses is built around creating places for the mentally ill to work. Once members have developed a sufficient track record they are encouraged to find employment in an unsheltered environment.

One obstacle that must be overcome is the fact that most Fountain House residents are on government disability. If they attain full-time work, they will lose their benefits. "Often people are ready for a full-time job but are hesitant because they are terrified of losing their benefits," reports Fountain House donor and board member Marlene Mieske. "Our goal is to help people attain independence, but it is an ongoing struggle with the way current government-benefit policies work."

Mieske says that "Fountain House does not focus on them as victims. It really focuses on asking the question, 'What are you going to do with your life?'" A psychiatric nurse herself, Mieske reports that most mental-health treatment programs are "just keeping people in a holding pattern. This is a program that moves people forward, if they're able to move. People are moving and changing and having opportunities. The focus is really on not the illness, but their potential—to be people, to have jobs, to get education."

Fountain House serves 1,300 members annually. It raises about $4½ million a year in private support, primarily from individuals, and pulls in another million and a half of revenue through program fees, product sales, and such. Nearly $11 million of government payments cover things like the supported housing.

"I've always felt we should make it more philanthropy and less government, because private philanthropy works in certain areas better than government," says Mieske. "Our costs are controlled because the most basic element of the program is members helping other members. The staff is there mostly as facilitators. We even have a large art gallery, open to the public, which is run by the members, not by staff. Almost everything that works at Fountain House is a result of members pitching in and taking responsibility for operations."

Fountain House has inspired similar organizations that serve more than 100,000 people annually. The group is willing to help founders create their own versions in additional cities and states.

Working Around Family Breakdown and Welfare Dependence

The most significant demographic transformation in the U.S. over the past five decades has been the revolution in family structure. It has also been one of the most detrimental for the welfare of children and the economic well-being of parents. In this chapter, we examine responses to the difficulties that single parents—most of them mothers—face in balancing custody of young children with the responsibilities of earning a family income. We then review some effective philanthropies that help Americans avoid single parenthood and organizations that strengthen fatherhood and male economic provision.

It is impossible to understand the struggles of single-parent homes without understanding a bit about how government welfare programs operate. The federal government spent around half a trillion dollars in 2013 on the top five welfare programs: Medicaid grants to the states ($267 billion), food stamps ($83 billion), the Earned Income Tax Credit ($55 billion), Supplemental Security Income ($51 billion), housing assistance ($50 billion), and payments to the states for Temporary Assistance for Needy Families ($21 billion). These numbers don't include other federal entitlements such as child nutrition subsidies, nor do they factor in the state portion of welfare payments, which are very large.

Even after the "workfare" reforms of the mid-1990s that reduced enrollments on America's traditional cash welfare program, dependence on government supports stands at historically high levels today. As economist Nicholas Eberstadt writes in *A Nation of Takers*:

> The habituation of Americans to life on entitlement benefits has already progressed much further than many of us might realize. As of 2009, an estimated 45 percent of all American children under 18 years were receiving at least one form of means-tested government aid.... An outright majority of Hispanic and African Americans of all ages were living in households reportedly using such programs, as well as almost 30 percent of Asian Americans and over 20 percent of non-Hispanic whites.

The influence of welfare payments on shifting norms of family has been profound. Most Americans agree that a social safety net is needed, but when benefits are ill-formulated or carelessly administered they can actually perpetuate problems. A priority for private philanthropists today is to build paths to individual responsibility and self-sufficiency that can counterbalance destructive effects of dependence on welfare transfers.

Considerable research has demonstrated that a growing marriage chasm, fueled by welfare dependence, is the leading factor separating strugglers and their children from economic and social success. "The United States is devolving into a separate-and-unequal family regime, where the highly educated and the affluent enjoy strong and stable households," while "unstable, unhappy, and unworkable" family structures are the pattern among the poor, summarizes Brad Wilcox, director of the National Marriage Project at the University of Virginia. "The primary way that those with low incomes can advance in the market economy is to get married, stay married, and work—but welfare programs have created incentives to do the opposite," conclude Michael Tanner and Tad DeHaven of the Cato Institute.

In addition to emphasizing the vital importance of marriage as the foundation for social success, philanthropists might put new emphasis on wealth accumulation by strugglers, suggest the authors of *When Helping Hurts*. "While public policy has historically encouraged wealth accumulation for middle-to-upper-class people, it has often discouraged wealth accumulation for the poor." Perverse incentives like the disability payments described earlier that penalize work would be an example.

The aspect of poverty that most concerns Americans is the way it crimps the horizons of innocent children. But one cannot effectively aid children without getting their parents involved. Even philanthropic investments in education, for instance, can be diluted and even cancelled, notes Donn Weinberg of the Harry and Jeanette Weinberg Foundation, if the child is coming home to a chaotic environment.

"If you truly want to help children, you must help the adults live in more sustainable ways," he suggests. This also sets a healthy model for the child. "When the kids see that their parent works, they think, 'When I grow up, I will work, because that's what mom does.' Philanthropic investments are muted unless we acknowledge this reality."

The problems of single-parent life

There are few domestic situations that produce more stress than raising young children alone. Yet there are far more single-parent families today than ever before.

- In 2013, 44 percent of all births in the U.S. took place out of wedlock; in 1963 that figure was just 7 percent.
- The median annual income for families headed by a single mother was $25,493 in 2012; the median income for all households was double that at $51,017.
- Two thirds of single mothers receive no child support from the fathers of their children.
- Nearly half of all single-parent families live below the poverty line; 42 percent of kids in single-parent households receive food stamps.
- One third of families maintained by women with no spouse present were unemployed in 2013, compared to less than 4 percent of married-couple families with children.

Raising children in two-parent families is challenging enough; demands are magnified in single-parent families enjoying fewer economic and emotional resources. We surveyed donors, charitable providers, and experts in moving strugglers from dependence to work, asking them what the biggest obstacles to self-support are among single parent families. This is what they told us:

- Having only a single income, which sometimes requires working multiple jobs.
- The necessity of paying for child care during the workday, and the difficulty of matching child care and work schedules.
- Having no help in completing household chores.
- Handling child nurture, discipline, homework, etc. alone.
- Lack of down time to recuperate, and economic margin to cover unexpected contingencies.
- Lack of time to pursue educational options that would help speed advancement.
- Social isolation due to a harried schedule and lack of time for either friendships or career networking.

A comprehensive approach to helping single mothers work

Due to the pressures on single parents, it can be easy for philanthropists to fall into the trap of simply providing short-term help rather than the hand up that will bring longer-term success. Including a clear path to gainful employment within the mix of assistance offered to single-parent strugglers is vital. Pressing needs like housing, utility payments, transportation costs, and groceries must be met to keep homes running. But skill building, work, and living patterns that foster work are most important overall.

A nonprofit that has managed to lead single mothers from debilitating dependence on public entitlements to rewarding independence is the Jeremiah Program based in Minneapolis, Minnesota. In the mid-1990s, when he was rector of the Basilica of Saint Mary in downtown Minneapolis, Michael O'Connell brought together a team of community leaders to seek solutions for low-income single parents. A donation of land by the company now known as Xcel Energy, and then a $5 million fundraising campaign, allowed the group to open its first residential building in 1998. By 2002, they had 39 housing units for single mothers and space for 66 children in a child-development center.

The Jeremiah Program serves low-income single mothers 18 and over who have graduated from high school or hold a GED. These women are often living without hope on public assistance, frequently with a history of neglect or abuse from the men in their lives. The goal of the program is to radically change these women's perceptions of themselves and their situations.

"To break out of poverty, there has to be a basic level of self-confidence," says Gloria Perez, who has led the Jeremiah Program since 1998. "If you are poor, there is a familiar safety net that you've known. It's hard to take risks and venture into new territory aimed at advancing yourself while clinging to that comfortable safety net. But when women see other women with the same kinds of barriers going through the same effort to break out of poverty, that is hugely beneficial. And when children see their mothers going to work, doing homework, and actively engaging in the community, the kids change."

It's hard to take risks and venture into new territory aimed at advancing yourself while clinging to that comfortable safety net.

Before becoming residents in the Jeremiah Program, single mothers must take an eight-week personal empowerment class. Once they move in, an additional eight weeks of the class follow. The campus-style housing is safe and fully furnished—but it isn't free. Women are required to pay 30 percent of their income for rent (averaging around $135 a month). In addition to their apartments they get playgrounds for their children, laundry facilities, and 24-hour security.

During their time as residents, mothers are required to attend weekly life-training that teaches parenting skills, health and wellness, personal financial literacy, and household independence. The program has on-site centers where children ages six weeks through preschool receive care while their mothers pursue education and career opportunities.

Career development is emphasized. Jeremiah Works! connects the women directly with area companies offering jobs, and women also enroll in local college programs. Residents get basic career counseling and steady encouragement to graduate out of the program. The average length of stay is three years.

Today, the Jeremiah Program serves 300 women and children annually at two sites in the Twin Cities area. Sister efforts recently opened in Austin, Texas, and in Boston. Donors in Fargo, North Dakota, are planning another site. The Frey Family Foundation of Minneapolis has been a cornerstone supporter, providing more than $2 million of general and expansion support, much of it in the form of matching challenge grants. "We give the highest possible marks to the Jeremiah Program in what they're doing," says president Jim Frey.

This campus-based, multifaceted, multiyear effort is costly. The Jeremiah Program's 2012 budget of $4.2 million translates to nearly $11,000 per family served each year. But by carefully selecting applicants who are ready to change their lives, and then offering strong programming, the effort has produced impressive results.

Data on women who graduated from the Jeremiah Program in 2012 and 2013 show that 40 percent earned a bachelor's degree, 54 percent completed an associate degree, and 6 percent completed an occupational certificate. When they came into the program these women were unemployed in 61 percent of the cases; the 39 percent who had some work were earning a little more than $9 per hour. After graduating, 77 percent were employed, at an average wage of $16.25 per hour; another 14 percent were finishing their education.

Working with welfare programs

In places where a comprehensive model like we've just examined is not practical or desirable, a donor might instead work with existing nonprofits that offer certain needed services. Donors might even get some of the comprehensive effect by investing in alliances between nonprofits that have distinct focuses—one on housing assistance, another on childcare, and a third on transportation. Mixing these with a solid workforce-training curriculum could yield powerful programming for helping single mothers.

Or donors might just want to keep a tight focus on work. The Center for Work Education and Employment in Denver may offer lessons. CWEE was founded in 1982 to help women transition to employment from the Aid to Families with Dependent Children program (the precursor to today's TANF welfare program). The passage of welfare reform in 1996 placed a lifetime limit of five years on the new TANF benefits, giving additional relevance to support for transitions to work. CWEE made it their mission to train recipients and help them find jobs.

Unlike other nonprofits in this chapter, CWEE works closely with the existing welfare system. Mothers are admitted to CWEE as a step in their process of transitioning off TANF. Like traditional work-boosting organizations, CWEE has three main planks: preparing for employment, finding employment, and keeping employment. Women attend classes for 30 hours per week—first a general orientation and then a ten-week career-readiness program that fills weekdays from 9 a.m. to 4 p.m.

Because over 50 percent of those who attend have no high-school diploma or GED, literacy skills are a cornerstone of the program. Depending on their skill level, participants might be placed in a GED-prep track or an adult basic-education track. Women learn foundational tech skills, including Internet use and word processing. Each applicant is required to give presentations to other students, CWEE staff, and guests to boost confidence and public speaking ability. Along the way, participants learn soft skills as well, get personalized counseling, and two years of follow-on help to improve job retention.

Being a welfare-to-work program, CWEE receives 60 percent of its funding from TANF funds that are tied to each woman who comes through. Remaining costs are covered by individual donors and foundations. In its early days, CWEE received linchpin backing from Colorado National Bank (now U.S. Bank), Excel Energy Company, and the Coors Foundation.

Manufacturing independence: the Women's Bean Project

Social enterprise—running a business with a moral mission—is a strategy that has also been used to help single mothers. Visitors to the Women's Bean Project warehouse in Denver will discover a nonprofit run like a mom-and-pop firm. On the warehouse's ground floor, there is a production line turning out packaged bean soups, baking mixes, coffees and teas, salsas and dips. Boxes of food line the walls, ready for sale.

The women who make and pack these products are mostly welfare mothers, former homeless, or individuals with addiction or criminal histories. "The women who come here have never experienced success," says project head Tamra Ryan. "The most significant change we see is that a woman who graduates from here leaves believing that she is worthy of a better life."

Jossy Eyre was a volunteer at a women's homeless shelter who noticed that the facility had many repeat customers who kept coming back. If women could be taught to work through actual on-the-job experience they would have a much better chance of a sustained life change, she reasoned, than if they were simply offered compensations for their poverty. She founded the Women's Bean Project in 1989, investing $500 of her own money and enlisting two homeless women to help create and sell Toni's Ten Bean Soup, WBP's first product.

From those humble origins, WBP's inventory has bloomed to three dozen food products produced and shipped from the Denver warehouse. These generate $1.2 million in annual revenue and employ about 70 troubled women per year. WBP merchandise is offered in 500 stores and 40 states across the country. Every Safeway and Kroger grocery store in Colorado carries their wares, as do online retailers Amazon, Overstock. com, and Walmart.com.

For a woman to get hired by the project, she can't have been employed for longer than a year at any point during her life. Yet she has to be at a point where she is now willing to sacrifice and work toward lasting life change. A multistep interview process helps to weed out unserious applicants. By the time a woman is hired, she has been required to show up four different times—punctually, and dressed appropriately. For every woman who is hired, four more apply and are turned down due to lack of readiness or capacity limitations in the program.

Once employed, the women work full-time for 38 hours per week for a total of nine months. Employees start on the production line. Later, they might transition to the reception desk or the shipping-and-receiving department. A maximum of 30 percent of paid time is allowed for classroom instruction or program activities. This includes technical training in computer use and finance. The emphasis is on actual work experience.

"You have to come to work every day on time, take direction, pay attention to detail, and communicate with your supervisor appropriately," says Ryan. "We hire people who, by definition, don't do these things well. They have all these barriers. But we get them to the point where they become good at what they do. And then it's time for them to leave, and we start all over again."

Unlike the Jeremiah Program, WBP doesn't directly provide services like housing and child care. The business does, however, link women with other resources that can help them meet those needs. Like CWEE, the Women's Bean Project helps fill a gap for women coming off TANF's five-year lifetime limit—a transition where not enough is being done to help women break away from harmful habits of dependence.

When a woman has achieved all of the competencies that WBP searches for, she is ready for graduation. On average, this happens nine to

12 months after a typical woman begins the program. One-hundred percent of graduates go on to other jobs, and six months after graduation, 85 percent are still employed.

Ryan has expanded the organization's base of donors from 45 in 2003 to over 5,000 by 2014. The Fox Family, Rose Community, and Denver foundations have been instrumental funders. Recently, contributed income has grown at a faster clip than sales, thanks to impressed donors. Nonetheless, WBP's database of 20,000 customers remains its most important long-term revenue base.

"We're appealing to both sides of the political aisle," Ryan notes. "If you're about social justice, we've got that. If you're about self-support and getting people off welfare, we're about that as well."

Bolstering marriage, fathering, and family functioning

A 2009 analysis of census data by the Brookings Institution concluded that adult Americans who followed "three elementary norms of growing up in modern society" can minimize their chances of falling into poverty to just 2 percent and increase their odds of landing in the middle class to a robust 74 percent. All they have to do is "finish high school, get a full-time job, and wait until age 21 and get married before having children." A solid marriage "remains America's strongest anti-poverty weapon," notes a report from the Heritage Foundation that finds that simply being married is enough to reduce by 82 percent the probability that your child will live in poverty.

A major difference between economically successful Americans and weak earners is that the successful tend to get married and work, while weak earners lag on both fronts. "Today, more than ever in the past, poor adults have children [before marrying], work only irregularly, and seldom marry at all," notes economist Lawrence Mead in *From Prophecy to Charity*. "Usually, the father disappears without paying child support, often due to failure to work. If the mother also fails to work, the family will end up on welfare."

A 2010 study by the Centers for Disease Control and Prevention concluded that children in two-parent families are less likely than single-parent counterparts to experience a wide array hardships. These include poor health, learning disabilities, attention deficit and hyperactivity disorder, inadequate health-care coverage, dental problems, and anti-social or disruptive behavioral.

Supporting organizations that help young people form stable marital unions, and that help preserve and strengthen marriages already made, is worthy philanthropy. Most such groups operate at a local level. One of the most successful is called First Things First.

First Things First was created in 1997 when leaders in Chattanooga, Tennessee, pooled their collective wisdom to fight what they saw as the greatest threat to their county: the breakdown of the family. The group has two primary goals: The first is to provide proven training and classes on how to succeed in marriage, parenting, and family life. Giving area residents the tools and skills they need to avoid problems in marriage, and nip them with effective interventions if they pop up, is at the heart of the nonprofit's work. A second goal is to build a more positive view of marriage in media, opinion, and culture. Young people are now often gun-shy about marriage and avoid it out of fear of divorce, says First Things First president Julie Baumgardner, sometimes because they were hurt by their own parents' breakup.

Simply being married is enough to reduce by 82 percent the probability that your child will live in poverty.

First Things First wouldn't have been possible without financial support and leadership from the Maclellan Family Foundation. "We realized that the city's biggest problem was the breakdown of families, and that every part of Chattanooga was being affected by it," president Hugh Maclellan, Jr. told *Philanthropy* magazine in 2003. Local leaders came to realize that "we could really make a difference in Chattanooga" by helping to reinforce families.

The group got nonprofits, churches, and government agencies working together. It convinced religious congregations to increase premarital preparation. It launched parenting classes for fathers and mothers. It went into city schools and publicized the advantages of family intactness for children and adults alike. It set up "lunch and learn" seminars inside workplaces. The group retrained local mental-health professionals on how to help endangered marriages. It partnered with hospitals on a Boot Camp for New Dads, and helped Head Start programs work material on the importance of fathering into their curricula. It assisted the county divorce court in establishing a divorce mediation project—requiring couples with small children to take a class where they learn about the effects of divorce on kids and requiring them to develop a post-divorce parenting plan.

Within a decade, the Chattanooga area had seen a 29 percent drop in divorce filings. Those that still take place are now far less likely to involve conflicts over custody and child support. Teen out-of-wedlock births have decreased 62 percent.

Sometimes informed and inspired by the success of First Things First and sometimes acting on their own, a number of other cities and funders have launched similar efforts. Interested funders including the WinShape Foundation (funded by the Cathy family), Terry and Mary Kohler (who have given more than $5 million in this area), the Annie E. Casey Foundation, the DeVos family, the Johnson Foundation, and others have promoted marriage preparation, pre-divorce intervention, parenting education, and fatherhood reinforcement regionally and nationally. A National Healthy Marriage Resource Center has arisen to coordinate efforts by such groups. Many of these organizations have very limited budgets, and there is a large upside for donors willing to invest. A somewhat dated but still useful resource on this subject is *Reviving Marriage in America: Strategies for Donors* by William Doherty, published by The Philanthropy Roundtable.

Working Around a Criminal History

In a given year, about 12 million Americans are arrested. About 1.2 million of these apprehensions are for violent crimes. There are approximately 2.3 million men and women incarcerated in the U.S. at any time.

Crime produces many social costs. One of these is that even after they have served their time, persons convicted of crimes will often remain unemployed. This increases the chances they will break the law again—hurting additional victims, ending up once again a charge of the state in prison, and being lost to society as a productive worker, taxpayer, contributing parent.

Of the 650,000 ex-offenders who are released from state and federal prisons each year (nine out of ten of them men) two thirds currently get rearrested within three years. Only a minority of prisoners have a solid familial support structure to fall back on after they walk out of prison. Lining up housing, getting loans, even acquiring a driver's license, can be tricky for an ex-convict. Many employers have understandable reservations about hiring former prisoners. So returning to familiar criminal patterns is an obvious risk.

If more released prisoners can be redirected to work and respectable citizenship, many negative social and economic consequences will be headed off. "The outcome of helping former prisoners become productive is overwhelmingly positive," says Texas donor Pat O'Brien. "Instead of costing the state money, these men can become successful, contributing members of society."

Already, many good workforce-development organizations have at least some guidance to offer on overcoming a crime record. That's because groups serving the hardest to employ know that past crimes are often part of the snarl of obstacles that have to be overcome on the path to self-support. Half to two thirds of the people who walk through the doors at many work nonprofits have some sort of criminal experience.

For instance, 60 percent of the men and women arriving at WorkFaith Connection (the Houston nonprofit inspired by Cincinnati Works) have a crime history. The most common convictions are drug-related; many women have a past in prostitution. The WorkFaith Connection staff encourage applicants to be honest with prospective employers about their record. Lying is never a solution, they counsel, while full disclosure and evidence of a new direction will inspire many employers to offer a second chance.

Similarly, 50 percent to 70 percent of the individuals who flow through Denver's Belay Enterprises have a criminal record. CEO James Reiner told us that convincing employers to hire a worker who has just completed a criminal sentence can be challenging, but that many companies are willing to look beyond a criminal record if the perpetrator has successfully held at least one job after his punishment. Helping an ex-offender build up that much-needed track record at a first workplace is often the key to a successful transition into the mainstream world.

Homeboy Industries, discussed in Chapter 5, does remarkable things with former gang members. Nearly all of its clients were involved in illegal activity. Many of them carry an official criminal record. Yet the group is able to redirect many into decent work.

Like Homeboy, Belay, and WorkFaith, other programs like Cara, StepUp, Taller San Jose, and America Works also help clients with criminal records as part of their wider efforts to reinforce work. Donors might consider supporting one of these existing programs by earmarking a grant to expand or deepen initiatives specifically serving ex-felons. Or a donor could focus narrowly on reaching former criminals, either by launching a new organization or adding a fresh track at a group already serving a complementary clientele.

Next in this chapter we will explore several donor-funded organizations that work inside and outside of prison walls to transform incarcerated criminals, assist their dependents, and guide former prisoners toward becoming useful workers.

Prison Entrepreneurship Program

While they face impediments, former criminals also sometimes have useful capabilities that can be tapped. Researchers have found that some ex-offenders have what it takes to be an entrepreneur: demonstrating independence, creativity, and resilience. Instead of using these qualities to cope with environmental stresses or to create criminal enterprises, as they may have in the past, there is potential for tapping these talents to succeed in small business. One analysis by management and entrepreneurship professor Matthew Sonfield of Hofstra University found that prisoners have nearly the same level of entrepreneurial skills as those classified as "fast-growth" entrepreneurs. If those skills can be directed down avenues that are legal and moral, the ex-offender may be able to not only support himself but become a competitive success.

One of the premier prison-to-work programs in the U.S. tries to tap latent entrepreneurial talents. The Prison Entrepreneurship Program is headquartered in Houston, with a second office in Dallas. Uniting businessmen and churches, it uses the concepts of entrepreneurship and moral responsibility to encourage men to remake their lives, in ways that will dramatically reduce their chances of returning to prison after leaving.

PEP starts with the belief that reaching prisoners while they are still locked up is a key to ushering them into fruitful work. Most workforce reentry programs only kick in after the cell door has swung open. PEP connects people still in lock-up with successful businessmen who can serve as mentors.

CEO Bert Smith explains that "Having someone whom prisoners perceive as wildly successful coming in from the outside and showing them some love is an incredible experience. It's not uncommon for us to have men in our program who have not had a visit from a family member for years. To have somebody who they don't know come in and spend an afternoon with them is really powerful. It can help them realize there is hope and a chance for a new start. We work from there."

PEP recruits from prisoners who are within three years of their release date. They can't have a sex-crime conviction, prison gang affiliation, or recent major disciplinary case. "We're really looking for men who have decided that they want to make a change," Smith says. "They just don't know how."

"Commitment to transformation is very important. It's about learning who you are. Admitting and learning from your mistakes in the past. And developing a plan to avoid those mistakes in the future," Smith continues. "We don't want men who are looking for the 'easy way out.' That's too often the mindset of the criminal. Personal transformation is hard work, and we're only interested in investing in those men who are willing to invest in themselves."

> Many ex-offenders have what it takes to be an entrepreneur: independence, creativity, resilience.

Inmates from any Texas prison can apply. Those accepted are transferred to one of two facilities. PEP's original home is the Cleveland Correctional Center, a medium-security, 520-bed facility about an hour north of Houston. The program's second unit, the Estes Correctional Facility near Dallas, began service in August 2014.

PEP participants are first enrolled in a three-month education track. It provides character training and basic skills development, like computer literacy. PEP's "Ten Driving Values," which reflect Judeo-Christian principles, provide a moral foundation for the program.

The cornerstone of PEP's instruction is the Business Plan Competition. Taught by PEP staff and business volunteers from the community, the course allows prisoners to plan high-quality entrepreneurial endeavors. The curriculum extends over six months, requires more than 1,000 hours of classroom time, hundreds of hours of homework, and offers college-level business training. It is offered twice a year to around 250 to 300 men each semester.

Each prisoner is paired with a volunteer business mentor who works with him on detailing his business vision. In addition to crafting the plan, each student must present and defend it in public. Inmates must make a 15-minute pitch to a panel of judges before they can graduate.

While prisoners are hard at work learning new life skills and mapping out a useful commercial enterprise, PEP is trying to build or renew a social structure for the prisoner to enter after his release. A prime goal of the program is reconciliation within the prisoner's family. That is a gigantically helpful factor in making a successful transition back to freedom, but it can be challenging, since most prisoners' families are fragmented and dysfunctional.

At the beginning of each semester, PEP collects contact information and then begins the process of finding family members and figuring out how best to communicate with them. They explain how the prisoner is working to turn his life around, and provide periodic updates on progress along the way. The goal is to have four family members attend the graduation ceremony for each man and see firsthand the changes he has made in his life.

Given its difficult population, PEP loses participants every semester. Some men drop out in the face of the difficult coursework. Others are expelled for behavioral violations. In the end, about 70 percent of the cohort who begin the program end up finishing.

PEP's services don't end after an inmate graduates, and certainly not after he leaves prison. There is evidence that the most vulnerable time for ex-offenders is the first few weeks after release. So PEP case managers pick up men on the day they are released and transport them to PEP-arranged transitional housing (for which the released person pays rent). Follow-up contact is ongoing. Graduates now living on their own can attend PEP's Entrepreneurship School, or eSchool. This offers a range of two- and three-hour workshops on all aspects of being in business—marketing, sales, accounting, management, and more. These workshops are also combined with business networking events.

While entrepreneurship is PEP's organizing principle, and a proven way of getting the attention of inmates, it isn't particularly the goal of the program to generate new businesses, and only a portion of graduates actually found them. PEP has identified 120 businesses started by the 850 individuals who have graduated since the organization was started in 2004. Most of these were one-man owner-operated firms.

PEP training, however, puts released prisoners in a good position to be hired by some existing business. Since mid-2010, every PEP graduate has secured a job within 90 days of his release. A recent survey of grads on the first anniversary of their release found 95 percent of them employed. Among average released prisoners, meanwhile, fully half are unemployed one year after getting out from behind bars.

Like other nonprofits helping struggling workers, one of PEP's key procedures is to form lasting relationships with businesses in a position to offer its graduates jobs. PEP has met the most success with small- to medium-sized owner-operated companies. "The key is to introduce the CEO to some of our graduates," says Smith. "That proves that they aren't wide-eyed animals. They're capable people ready to go to work, and in the vast majority of cases, very personable."

As good as PEP's job results are, what may be its most important result is non-economic. A careful, controlled analysis by Baylor University found that just 7 percent of 2009 PEP graduates had returned to crime after three years—while the three-year recidivism rate of all persons released from Texas prisons was 23 percent rate. In its ability to reduce the flow of released inmates back into illegal activity, PEP also beat every other one of the nine best rehabilitation programs run in Texas prisons. Finally, the Baylor researchers compared PEP graduates to former prisoners who had qualified for PEP but then gotten paroled before they had a chance to participate. This confirmed that PEP cuts the recidivism rate of its participants to less than a third of the level it would otherwise reach.

Strikingly, PEP is solely funded by donors and manned largely by executive, MBA, and church volunteers. One of PEP's current philanthropic supporters is the Rockwell Fund. CEO Terry Bell says that early on, his foundation was not convinced that the PEP model would work. But the thoroughness with which PEP screens for the right applicants impressed the fund, and when they saw the data on the drop in recidivism they were sold. "PEP has done a great job of keeping people out of jail and giving them what they need most: the opportunity to become employed," says Bell.

One ex-prisoner who came through the program and is now working as an instructor and fundraiser for WorkFaith Connection in Houston is Scott Wesley. "For me, the job was the icebreaker to ultimately reenter my children's lives, provide health insurance and child-support payments for them, get my driver's license again, and begin saving for retirement," he explains. "These are little things that normal people do that make you feel a part of society. It begins with a job. That job is an entry point on so many levels."

"Nothing speaks to the Prison Entrepreneurship Program's success more powerfully than a single statistic," argued a recent piece in the *Houston Chronicle*: "30 percent of the program's donors in recent years are graduates. From felon to philanthropist—that's a transformation worthy of support." Two thirds of the PEP staff are also former inmates.

Center for Employment Opportunities

Headquartered in New York City with a presence extending around the country, the Center for Employment Opportunities is a nonprofit with a big footprint in the area of prisoner reentry. CEO has used local philanthropic support to add four new sites in upstate New York, three in California, and two in Oklahoma over the last half-dozen years.

CEO was founded by the Vera Institute of Justice as a demonstration project. Unlike PEP, which works both in prison and outside prison, CEO focuses on persons who have recently left lockup and are seeking work. CEO staff members collaborate with parole and probation officers to find the best participants for the program. "Those first 90 days are when people are most motivated, when they most need a job, but when it's hardest to find a job," says Sam Schaeffer, CEO's executive director.

Former inmates practice good work skills in real jobs: showing up on time, cooperating with the supervisor and co-workers. At the end of each shift they are paid, so we're drawing an immediate link between effort and outcome.

CEO places special emphasis on working with former prisoners between the ages of 18 to 25. These young adults haven't had a whole life of crime, so there are better chances to redirect them into law-abiding work. Unlike the vast majority of successful job programs, CEO doesn't screen intensively for a transformative attitude. If ex-offenders want a job, and are willing to show up for CEO's orientation, then they are in. They are given multiple opportunities—if they drop out, they can come back later.

CEO's New York City program begins with one week of life-skills education to ground participants in the fundamentals of being an employee. Then participants get a pair of steel-toed boots and a work ID, and they immediately begin to work on CEO's social enterprise: a maintenance and janitorial service that works in city agencies. In New York City alone, CEO now maintains 45 work crews. Branches in other areas run similar social ventures. In Tulsa, for instance, CEO workers work in recycling facilities and clean a community college. The revenues from these businesses subsidize the program.

"Former inmates practice good work skills in real jobs: showing up on time, cooperating with the supervisor and co-workers. At the end of each shift they are paid, so we're drawing an immediate link between effort and outcome. They're also being evaluated on these basic work behaviors," Schaeffer explains.

Ex-offenders carry out this transitional work four days per week. On the fifth day they return to CEO offices for job instruction and counseling. Once a former inmate has demonstrated readiness to transition to a private-sector job, the staff begins to work with him on finding opportunities and arranging interviews. After placement in a job, the organization offers up to a year of services to keep things on track and suggest ways to advance.

CEO's expansion to California was partially funded by grants from REDF and from the Edna McConnell Clark Foundation. When the organization moved into Oklahoma it got aid from the George Kaiser Family Foundation. Additional expansion is possible with philanthropic help.

RIDGE renews family relationships to build responsibility

Many of the people behind bars today have family members in the world outside who are in a position to suffer or prosper in tandem with them. The Sentencing Project reports that in 2009 more than 1.7 million children in the U.S. had an incarcerated parent. Linking these parents (most of them men) to work as soon as possible can have beneficial effects not only for the former prisoner but also for related women and children. Conversely, a released prisoner with a family support system is more likely to be successful economically, and to stay out of prison.

Headquartered in Ohio, the RIDGE Project works to retain and renew the relationships between prisoners and their families and to build on constructive overlaps between social success and job success. It has found a significant overlap in the skills that make a good spouse and parent and those that make a good employee and worker. Their "family first" approach has attracted donors who are interested in tackling the twin problems of joblessness among ex-offenders and their lack of involvement in their children's lives.

The RIDGE Project works to bolster fathering capacities and ambitions among incarcerated men, and then set them on a career path that can help them be a provider when they are released. "We work to stabilize the relationship, and then out of healthy families, we work to move them into workforce development," says Cathy Tijerina, who co-founded the RIDGE Project with her husband, Ron, in the early 1990s. Ron was incarcerated for more than 15 years, so they speak from direct experience about the challenges of rebuilding lives after a criminal conviction. "What we've learned is that you can have all the skill in the world, but if you don't have any character then you're prone to continue in a cycle of destruction," adds Ron Tijerina.

The RIDGE Project has three areas of focus: prevention, intervention, and redirection. The prevention element works with young people, mostly in schools, to help them avoid getting into trouble in the first place. Intervention focuses on fathers who are incarcerated or who are ex-offenders, strengthening their ties with family and connecting them to work. Redirection focuses on developing character and healthy habits and a positive mindset among prisoners.

> You can have all the skill in the world, but if you don't have character you're prone to continue in a cycle of destruction.

Currently, the RIDGE Project works in 21 of Ohio's 28 prisons. In its classes, the project uses the Latin concept of the "Tyro"—meaning a beginner or novice, but also describing a new warrior. There is a "rite of passage" emphasis, and encouragement of Tyro fraternities that use ex-cons to encourage and guide men coming through the system behind them. This helps graduates hold onto the life changes they have experienced and gives new trainees models they can believe in.

Tyro programming runs from nine to 18 weeks in different versions. About 80 classes are offered every week, inside and outside prisons. These aim to build new warriors who can succeed in life by strengthening their family, taking responsibility, and becoming financially able.

After completing this personal training, inmates participate in workforce instruction. This includes job ethics, plus specific vocational training. For instance, RIDGE has partnered with a trucking company to offer inmates classroom work leading to a commercial driver's license. There is a welding track and one in the culinary arts. When inmates leave prison RIDGE helps place them in appropriate jobs.

RIDGE preps prisoners for hard realities. "We help them understand that, yes, they will have to work harder and they will have to prove themselves longer," says Cathy Tijerina. "We help reinvent these men, who would otherwise be undesirable, unemployable, and unreliable," says her husband. "The Tyro program creates a rite of passage that moves them from a learned helplessness to the great 'what if?' They become capable of being successful."

The results: 270 men employed after completing the Tyro program, at an average wage of $13.14 per hour, with a 71 percent job retention rate after three months. The organization has a waiting list of 5,000 Ohio prisoners who want to participate. Word of mouth is the main way the organization advertises its services.

Some more models

We'll close this chapter by listing a few other programs that donors might investigate when looking for models to help former prisoners enter working life. (And don't forget the work-building charities mentioned in previous chapters—like Homeboy Industries and Taller San Jose—that have special focuses on strugglers with criminal pasts.)

- Specific prisons often have their own particular work programs. Some of these are very distinctive. The Sing Sing Correctional Facility located on the Hudson River north of New York City, for instance, has a program that allow inmates who have graduated from college to earn a master's degree in theology. The program was created by the New York Theological Seminary in 1982, and since then more than 400 men have graduated. About 15 students participate each year in the one-year, 36-credit-hour course, which is 100-percent scholarship funded. Similar specialized degrees could be offered in other prisons, with donor support.

- Prison Fellowship is a nonprofit that provides a wide range of services to help prisoners redirect their lives in more constructive directions, thanks to about $40 million of annual private support. It offers Christian counseling and services to inmates while they are locked up, assistance for inmate families, and re-entry guidance. Many of its efforts help local churches become involved in mentoring and assisting former prisoners in their area as they are released and in need of housing, jobs, and accountability.

- For the majority of released prisoners who are not involved in an intensive support program, simply knowing where to look for work is often the biggest struggle in starting their new life. A nonprofit called the Next Step has organized COFFE to help solve this problem. The Cooperative of Felon-Friendly Employers provides a national database of businesses that are willing to hire felons. It helps aid transitions by matching ex-cons, employers, and parole organizations.

- There are programs that are focused specifically on young people. Getting Out and Staying Out, founded in New York City by a retired business executive, works with minors and young adults ages 16 to 24. It has produced low rates of re-incarceration, with generous support from individual donors in the business world, and foundations like Achelis & Bodman. Fresh Lifelines for Youth in California is another organization that works to redirect kids who have become involved in the criminal justice system.

Investment
Opportunities

Although there are many well-established charities connecting economic strugglers with productive work, there remains much untilled ground in this area. Donors have many opportunities to expand on what has already been built, to transfer working models to new locations, to create specialized programs that serve particular population niches.

Whatever your interests and finances as a donor, there are excellent options for investing in expansion of America's working population. Indeed, donors who support work will often find it is the very best way to cement and extend their other charitable achievements in low-income communities. If you fund addiction recovery, why not parlay that into help with career advancement for those with a history of substance abuse? If homeless ministry is an interest, there are few more permanent solutions than helping this troubled population go to work. If reducing crime is one of your priorities, workforce development should be one of your tools.

Whether you are considering extending an existing organization or supporting a homegrown effort, it is always helpful to recruit business partners and philanthropic allies early on. The Weinberg Foundation's Marci Hunn says a healthy mix of partners can vastly increase success rates. The John William Pope Foundation of Raleigh, North Carolina, used its twenty-fifth anniversary celebration to rally other local advocates around StepUp Ministry. Around 500 attendees at their 2011 banquet raised nearly $300,000 and kickstarted the ministry to a new level.

Supporting research in this area is another worthwhile option. The Texas-based Miles Foundation recently approved a multiyear grant that links Catholic Charities of Fort Worth with the University of Notre Dame Lab for Economic Opportunities in a partnership that seeks "to reduce poverty in America through rigorous academic research and evaluation of anti-poverty programs" with a special "focus on methods to increase entrepreneurship in implementation of poverty relief services." The Miles Foundation committed $250,000 to the project through 2017.

If your philanthropic interests fall within the education arena, explore ways to create strong pathways to work within schools that serve lots of lower-income children. Some charter schools emphasize occupational skills and have the administrative nimbleness to work with donors to customize programs. Following is an assortment of avenues that philanthropists might follow, sifted by budget level. These are merely meant to be suggestive, and to encourage you to find your own course of assistance.

Annual support of $1,000–$100,000
- Serve on the board of a promising work-building charity.
- Fund a single struggling individual with whom you have a church, business, or other connection that provides social support, so he or she can attend job training and turn his or her life around in the process.
- Fund a single struggling individual with whom you have a church, business, or other connection that provides social support, so he or

she can attend a drug or alcohol recovery program that emphasizes work training.

- Work with one of the many business- or church-based programs that link newly released prisoners with mentors who can help them adjust to working life.
- Sign up your business, and the businesses of colleagues, with some of the many nonprofits that match newly trained strugglers with firms needing entry-level employees.
- Seek out ways to publicize the value of private action in support of workforce development. This could be through fraternal and business groups, public forums, local publications, social media, conventions, and other avenues.
- Educate fellow philanthropists on why workforce development is a worthy investment area for donors. A good way to spark interest might be a tour of a local nonprofit doing excellent work.
- Fund advocacy organizations that promote work as a means of escaping poverty.
- Support the general operations of a job-training group in your geographic region.
- If social enterprises interest you, there are many opportunities for helping nonprofits organize ventures that can provide locally useful labor and services while also giving strugglers a first successful experience in the working world.
- Bring a Jobs for Life chapter to your church. If one already exists, consider ways that you as a donor can make it even more effective by contributing either knowledge or money.
- Consider a grant to help Jobs for Life expand to more cities.
- Make a five-year commitment to fund a specific, valuable position. For instance, the Cara Program's socio-emotional skills trainer is among the organization's most critical and difficult-to-fill posts. Cincinnati Works' legal coordinator helps people resolve court issues hindering job acquisition and retention.
- Earmark a grant to specifically help a workforce-development organization meet tricky labor-law requirements imposed by the federal government.
- Give with the aim of helping a workforce-development outfit purchase more up-to-date equipment, software, or curricula, or help them create a better website or job-matching database.
- Fund nonprofits such as Vehicles for Change, Ways to Work, or the

Lift Garage that help workers obtain and maintain cars or other reliable means of transportation to and from their jobs.

- Pull together data in your community to uncover growing and worker-constrained economic sectors, then consider building or supporting organizations that can train non-employed locals to meet these business needs.
- Earmark a grant to help an existing work-related nonprofit better evaluate its own results: number of individuals employed, length of employment, and quality of jobs, so that these outcomes can be monitored and improved over time.
- Fund apprenticeships and vocational training for low-income individuals. Focus on the trades, where there has been an erosion of pathways into employment.
- Offer a matching grant to help your local workforce-development nonprofit motivate other givers.
- Inspire lapsed major donors, colleagues, and friends by offering to personally match their new gifts to work-building charities.
- Pick a work-building charity you trust and then fund the hiring of a communications consultant who can help them get their story out to potential supporters.
- Commission a feasibility study for turning a top-tier local or regional workforce-development organization into a national organization.
- Fund organizations that expose at-risk students to workforce successes early on.
- Support summer jobs and paid internships for at-risk students.
- Work to keep excellent vocational education on the docket for young people. At a time when many helping organizations are defining success exclusively in terms of college education, there remain many students for whom a more hands-on work-first approach will be most effective.
- Organize mentoring networks and fund mentorship organizations in your local area to interest at-risk young people in work and careers.
- Invest in a school that has a focus on developing practical work skills in young people from troubled backgrounds. Charter schools are generally much easier to work with than conventional school bureaucracies.
- Ignite the entrepreneurial instincts of young people with a gift to a school that has an entrepreneurial training track (such as Pro-Vision) or start one at a local school you already support.

- Offer entrepreneurial inspiration and training for the young through one of the many independent nonprofits that do this, from Junior Achievement on down.
- Recognizing the special barriers that single parents face, consider funding nonprofits that link work with assistance in housing and child care.
- Support groups that encourage marriage and strengthen or rebuild lower-income families; this can help reduce the flow into household forms that make work very difficult.
- On an individual level, find a single-parent family with whom you have a church, business, or other connection that provides social support and help them find pathways to work.
- If you are a business owner, explore ways that you could integrate job training and hiring for struggling populations into your own commercial needs.
- Help publicize the benefits of work-focused programs for ex-offenders, including much lower rates of repeat crime and reincarceration.
- Support programs that tap the entrepreneurial instincts of former gang leaders, drug dealers, and other convicts to interest them in legitimate business and work.
- Invest in research on job pathways for the mentally ill, an area that gets scant attention.
- Publicize the pernicious effects of today's explosion of disability support at the expense of meaningful work.
- Fund pilot programs that experiment ways of pulling the disabled from dependence to work and self-reliance.
- Work within the business world to create more willingness among hiring managers to treat as a potential resource persons who have recently received nonprofit remedial training after a previous spotty work history.
- Fund a high-quality annual report for an excellent workforce nonprofit to help them communicate better with prospective supporters.
- In all of this, take advantage of your existing local community structures—don't reinvent the wheel, but establish partnerships with existing nonprofits, churches, business leagues, and civic organizations.

Investments of $100,000–$500,000
- Strive to double the number of participants in some good workforce-development program.
- In cities with many clients in need of work training but high

nonprofit costs due to expensive rents and other factors, help effective organizations reach a critical mass where it is easier to support themselves.

- Support venture philanthropies that invest in social enterprises where strugglers can build good work histories—like REDF, the Tipping Point Community, or the Robin Hood Foundation.
- Target a gift to some less appealing area of an effective nonprofit's work. For example, unglamorous but important building repairs.
- Find an organization where you trust the mission, model, and management enough to offer a large general-operating grant. General-operating funds are the essential base that keeps nonprofits operating and healthy.
- Make a three-year commitment to help a successful nonprofit add some new, previously unserved population of strugglers into their work training.
- Divide among several different social ventures a grant that allows them to share information and tactics, so they can become better at what they do.
- Help an existing workforce-bolstering group launch an initiative specifically aimed at single parents that includes an effective, albeit expensive, residential component.
- Help some training nonprofit conduct a randomized, controlled study to analyze its approach and results.
- Provide funds so job-training nonprofits can build partnerships with local community colleges or vocational organizations.
- Offer a multiyear gift to help your local gospel rescue mission expand its pathways to employment for the homeless, addicted, and mentally ill.

Investments of $500,000 or more
- If no effective charity linking strugglers to work exists in your region, launch one.
- Fund the expansion of an exemplary existing organization into new geographic territory.
- Invest in the creation of new social enterprises run by nonprofits that can offer positions to previously failed workers, along with revenues that can be plowed back into more job training.
- With a larger gift, create a network linking social enterprises across the country—a clearinghouse that can help these ventures learn

from each other and publicize their successes at serving both struggling workers and local businesses with employee gaps.

- Invest in the infrastructure of an impressive workforce charity—like the new building that has opened many avenues for the Life Learning Center in northern Kentucky.

- Fund a documentary or deep academic research effort that can illustrate the successes and anti-poverty potential of tough-love work training by charitable organizations.

And so forth.

We've surveyed in this book a range of approaches to reinforcing work: direct-training models, efforts that put a heavy emphasis on classroom instruction, social ventures that plunk people into actual positions, mentoring approaches, and many others. The opportunities in this area for imaginative philanthropists are boundless.

Despite the impressive work of many workforce-development charities already in existence, the impact of these organizations is a drop in the bucket when viewed from a national perspective. As much as one fifth of the U.S. working-age population is either unemployed or underemployed. There are many more economic strugglers who could benefit from tough-minded yet supportive job assistance.

Success in this area can dramatically change the physical conditions and psychological health of legions of families. It can also help local economies. And a kind of upward virtuous spiral can ensue when serious emphasis is put on work. Buckling down on a job can beget success which begets more initiative, which begets more success, which then influences children in the family, and so on.

"This is an exciting area" for funders, says Donn Weinberg of the Weinberg Foundation, "an area you can measure easily and get a lot of personal satisfaction from." Work doesn't just banish poverty; it can "bring satisfaction and significance" to unhappy lives, notes Hugh Whelchel of the Institute for Faith, Work, and Economics. "Nothing," summarizes philanthropist David Weekley, "creates more self-respect and sets a family on its way better than having good work to do."

INDEX

ABOUT THE PHILANTHROPY ROUNDTABLE

The Philanthropy Roundtable is America's leading network of charitable donors working to strengthen our free society, uphold donor intent, and protect the freedom to give. Our members include individual philanthropists, families, corporations, and private foundations.

Mission

The Philanthropy Roundtable's mission is to foster excellence in philanthropy, to protect philanthropic freedom, to assist donors in achieving their philanthropic intent, and to help donors advance liberty, opportunity, and personal responsibility in America and abroad.

Principles

- Philanthropic freedom is essential to a free society
- A vibrant private sector generates the wealth that makes philanthropy possible
- Voluntary private action offers solutions to many of society's most pressing challenges
- Excellence in philanthropy is measured by results, not by good intentions
- A respect for donor intent is essential to long-term philanthropic success

Services

World-class conferences

The Philanthropy Roundtable connects you with other savvy donors. Held across the nation throughout the year, our meetings assemble grantmakers and experts to develop strategies for excellent local, state, and national giving. You will hear from innovators in K–12 education, economic opportunity, higher education, national security, and other fields. Our Annual Meeting is the Roundtable's flagship event, gathering the nation's most public-spirited and influential philanthropists for debates, how-to sessions, and discussions on the best ways for private individuals to achieve powerful results through their giving. The Annual Meeting is a stimulating and enjoyable way to meet principled donors seeking the breakthroughs that can solve our nation's greatest challenges.

Breakthrough groups

Our Breakthrough groups—focused program areas—build a critical mass of donors around a topic where dramatic results are within reach. Breakthrough groups become a springboard to help donors achieve lasting effects from their philanthropy. Our specialized staff of experts helps grantmakers invest with care. The Roundtable's K–12 education program is our largest and longest-running Breakthrough group. This network helps donors zero in on today's most promising school reforms. We are the industry-leading convener for philanthropists seeking systemic improvements through competition and parental choice, administrative freedom and accountability, student-centered technology, enhanced teaching and school leadership, and high standards and expectations for students of all backgrounds. We foster productive collaboration among donors of varied ideological perspectives who are united by a devotion to educational excellence.

A powerful voice

The Roundtable's public-policy project, the Alliance for Charitable Reform (ACR), works to advance the principles and preserve the rights of private giving. ACR educates legislators and policymakers about the central role of charitable giving in American life and the crucial importance of protecting philanthropic freedom—the ability of individuals and private organizations to determine how and where to direct their charitable assets. Active in Washington, D.C., and in the states, ACR protects charitable giving, defends the diversity of charitable causes, and battles intrusive government regulation. We believe the capacity of private initiative to address national problems must not be burdened with costly or crippling constraints.

Protection of donor interests

The Philanthropy Roundtable is the leading force in American philanthropy to protect donor intent. Generous givers want assurance that their money will be used for the specific charitable aims and purposes they believe in, not redirected to some other agenda. Unfortunately, donor intent is usually violated in increments, as foundation staff and trustees neglect or misconstrue the founder's values and drift into other purposes. Through education, practical guidance, legislative action, and individual consultation, The Philanthropy Roundtable is active in guarding donor intent. We are happy to advise you on steps you can take to ensure that your mission and goals are protected.

Must-read publications

Philanthropy, the Roundtable's quarterly magazine, is packed with useful and beautifully written real-life stories. It offers practical examples, inspiration, detailed information, history, and clear guidance on the differences between giving that is great and giving that disappoints. We also publish a series of guidebooks that provide detailed information on the very best ways to be effective in particular aspects of philanthropy. These guidebooks are compact, brisk, and readable. Most focus on one particular area of giving—for instance, teaching, charter schools, support for veterans, anti-poverty programs, and other topics of interest to grant makers Real-life examples, hard numbers, management experiences of other donors, recent history, and policy guidance are presented to inform and inspire savvy donors.

Join the Roundtable!

When working with The Philanthropy Roundtable, members are better equipped to achieve long-lasting success with their charitable giving. Your membership in the Roundtable will make you part of a potent network that understands philanthropy and strengthens our free society. Philanthropy Roundtable members range from Forbes 400 individual givers and the largest American foundations to small family foundations and donors just beginning their charitable careers. Our members include:

- Individuals and families
- Private foundations
- Community foundations
- Venture philanthropists
- Corporate giving programs
- Large operating foundations and charities that devote more than half of their budget to external grants

Philanthropists who contribute at least $100,000 annually to charitable causes are eligible to become members of the Roundtable and register for most of our programs. Roundtable events provide you with a solicitation-free environment.

For more information on The Philanthropy Roundtable or to learn about our individual program areas, please call (202) 822-8333 or e-mail main@PhilanthropyRoundtable.org.

ABOUT THE AUTHOR

Journalist David Bass previously served as a grants officer and communications director at the John William Pope Foundation in North Carolina, where he focused on nonprofits involved in workforce development. Prior to that he was an editor and reporter with the John Locke Foundation, where he covered state General Assembly sessions and other issues. He has a journalism degree from Thomas Edison State College, and lives in North Carolina with his wife.